WARS
OF THE
MIND

VOLUME 5:
(*Between Flesh & Bone.*)

By: Jonathan *W.* Haubert

Edited By: Jonathan W. Haubert

8   X   8

Order this book online at www.trafford.com
or email orders@trafford.com

Most Trafford titles are also available at major online book retailers.

Printed in the United States of America.

ISBN: 978-1-4907-2180-4 (sc)
ISBN: 978-1-4907-2181-1 (e)

Library of Congress Control Number: 2013923120

Trafford rev. 04/15/2014

Trafford
PUBLISHING®   www.trafford.com
North America & international
toll-free: 1 888 232 4444 (USA & Canada)
fax: 812 355 4082

NO RETURN

(COUNT YOUR DEAD)

Wars of the Mind Contents:

<u>Chapter 4</u> – *Ending the World*

Chapter 1

Seeping Deeper

Terminate

Thrust headfirst into the beginning of the end.
Drive all the fears back and admit that we are sins.
Breakdown all what holds that greater meaning.
Destroy anything that stands now in our way.

Then all is set and ready for another epic chapter.
An ongoing rant within this chronicle of pain.
Stand now so very tall and then you shall reach it.
The other side of the beginning which now must end.

Thrust much deeper beyond all that has yet to be stated.
We are standing on the line now, here below the waves.
We are all so very ready now, to see the darkness beyond the light.
We shall all together terminate, the ending that has now begun...
"Onward pushing, into the wars of our minds."

Bending The Flame

I can feel it dancing in the palm of my hand.
I can feel it growing so distorted with rage.
As so deeply confused, for what remains unseen.
I can feel it burning, and that is my fate indeed.

I was hoping that you might not see it.
I was hoping that we just might someday forget.
I can't but let go and watch us all die.
I know now the truth, and it lies hidden in time.

You were screaming at the top of your lungs.
You were bleeding red teardrops from your eyes.
You were so happy when I wasn't there.
You had sent me to hell, to burn in torment.
I can feel the flames bending, here in the palms of my hands.
And I know now *"I am back..."*

Nightmares Under My Bed

As mother whispered her soothing lullaby into my head.
All that remained was hours upon hours of pure dreaming.
It was so very brilliant, all the innocent thoughts of joy.
Then all at once, dark clouds began to flood the beautiful skies.

No matter how hard I had ever tried to change it.
Still to this day I cannot escape all my tormented fears and pains.
Please mother come now and save your child, here weeping so cold.
It is so dark out now and I believe that my soul is lost.

As all night long, for hours - there tossing and turning with rage.
Was such a bitter cause, all the disappointments of the past.
Still to this day I can feel it, as all emotions are numbed out.
At one point there might have been hope, but now this is all that's left.

Please mother try to wake me, before the demons eat my soul.
Please God protect me, here as the Devil takes his hold.
Please somebody try to save me, from all the nightmares under my bed.
Please just help me to admit it, "that it is but all inside my head..."

As I Promised

As I had promised, I will be there to catch you as you fall.
Into the darkness, "*it calls out to admire the soothing echoes.*"
As all to be so grim, here in the conclusion of our ends.
Exceeded and we're at the true point *which was never fully noticed.*
And I did promise, that I would be there to save the day.
Then all behind my eyes is perceived as such a great nonsense.
And as I had once said, I shall love you even passed death.
For all yet to come and still yet to know.
Found hidden beneath a frozen lake, there in our souls.
It floods all the pools, of the insanity beyond my heart.
As I had promised, I will be there to fall as you laugh.
Into the darkness, of all our lies that did never exist.
I did promise, that I would pull the trigger with a smile.
Then thrust between the shadows, "*and it's all just in my head.*"
As I promised, I shall always love you, "*even passed death...*"

"*So please now awake...*"

Crucifix In Blood

Sinking deeper, into the endless void in the back of my head.
Come then and cut open the roof of my mouth in spite.
Let us both watch as all my sins bleed forth and flood the lands.
It is upon the Devil's wishes that we shall leap over the ledge.
A smile then given, for we are soon to come to an end.
It felt so Goddamn terrific, as gallons of blood bled from my heart.
Was once a sad child, *there screaming at me from the other side of the mirror.*
Then as the moon wept I knew that it was our true end.
For now can never it be achieved, and there will be no second chance.
Then left there in the middle of the wrist, *a message of pain from that love.*
It was all so great and now but a miss, left weeping alone in fear.
Can never we save us from ending like that, so very dull and bleak.
Now there submerged, that rusted crucifix in blood.
Does it have some greater meaning, or only the obvious sense?
Come please and take me away, so at that point we erase today.
As tomorrow dies and fades to gray, we are then left with but only this to say.
"The end has come, but I do believe that we are ready..."

Nearing Cashed

So scream for me, come bleed for me.
Laugh my love for we are dying now.
Come pull my strings, come turn the switch.
For now in flames and forgotten again.

It's nearing cashed, now just burning ash.
It tastes like death with a hint of spirits.
We're just reaching now, still reaching now.
Hoping we might float away to the stars.

So scream for me, come bleed for me.
Run all you wish, for never shall we grasp.
The smoke it floods, consuming our dreams.
Now nearing cashed, just burning ash.
"Then we wake up alone, dead in our dreams..."

Like Pawns

Un-illustrated minds breaking, because the drug was just that great.
Dire gambles taken, then cast back and brutally thrown away.
I am but "that fucking demon" or whatever kind of monster you make of me.
Please do not misquote my meaning, "I truly am just that evil."

Like a dreamer, reaching out into the abyss of my mind.
Like a child, left alone in pain with only fear to keep me in check.
We were like pawns, just so easily cast out and forgotten.
Then when the world came to an end, it was I that laughed and smiled...

Un-forgiven natures hindering, for we are now at the dawn of our ends.
Like pawns we were cast aside, without even a second chance.
I was once a human, a man that tried to save our world.
I am here and now but a demon, laughing as we all burn...
" We are nothing but FUCKING PAWNS!!!"

Hungry For Flesh

I am starving here, so very hungry for flesh.
I want to watch the world end, within my own two hands.
I need to just scream-laughing, then regurgitate the frozen ash.
God I am *FUCKING* starving, so damn hungry for human flesh...

Feed me please and show to our lord that *we can* be saved.
Try your best to believe in the lie, there dancing upon your breath.
Tilt then back, to let the nonsense consume the line.
I must feed soon, or I believe that I might die...

I am so starving now, so very-very hungry for flesh.
I want now to hold the world in my hands, *and then laugh as it ends.*
I must be the bad guy, the fuck-up that can never be.
I will soon achieve what I seek, "and on your flesh I shall feast..."

I must feed – I must feed.

Drive the Needle

Drive the needle into my eyes.
Inject the poison until I go blind.
Blind to the fact in which we all hate.
The love of pure insanity which now stands sane.

Fuck me vicious, until I have no soul that remains.
Drive that bullet, right through the middle and into my brain.
Take my ashes and swallow them down.
Then open your eyes for truly I am you...

Drive the needle into my eyes.
Retract the glory that was once my mind.
Lead me over and into the waking truth of this world.
Let us go now, far beyond the other side of then.

So hate me fully, for I have disgraced all mankind.
When on that day I had murdered my only true love.
Please just end me here, at this tormented moment in time.
Inject all your hatred, into this once blissful mind...

Come drive the needle into my heart.
Inject my body with but only ash and tar.
You cannot save me, for I do wish to remain damned.
Oh please drive the needle, into the center of my spine once again.

It Cuts In Deep

I feel so weak, lying - bleeding on the floor.
I want to sleep, to erase the memories of that whore.
I want to cut, all of those thoughts out of my head.
I need to wake up, and then try to prove that I'm not dead.
I do feel so weak, crying - weeping on the floor.
I want to wake up, and live not such a repetitive bore.
I know this chapter is turning, *something new on its way*.
In hell my soul is burning, but with that thought I feel okay.
It cuts in deep, into *the Past* that I once thought I had left behind.
I am so weak, lying on the floor, "bleeding – crying..."

Played Again

I am but only a fragmented recollection of our past.
Played again, for I had the audacity to glance back.
To watch _my world_ burn, and become just a forgotten _planet of ash._
Then as all our memories go, we need today to but only laugh.

"So scream my love," we have arrived here now at the end.
Drink it down as our minds flood, growing upon sadistic whims.
We reach out weeping, "_please mother save us from the dark._"
I feel so played again, and it's the same like all the many times before.

So abstract! _This mind that is trying to forgive the harsh lesson of then._
So we are dead! _And it is the same but only with a little less sin._
So what the Fuck! _Can we here and now just let go and then fall away?_
So I've been played again! "_But this was never a fucking game!_"

As She Gropes My Heart

Then it was a better, chance to free all of my tormented thoughts.
As when she spoke my name, now forgotten and with time was lost.
Who are we? The ones scratching at the surface but yet never to gain.
All of this life was spent searching, and still it continues _beyond the grave._

Then as all my life was fleeting, I had opened my eyes so painful to see.
She was never truly an angel, but still to this day _I wish that I could believe._
But she is just a demon, groping my heart there damned to hell.
Still the reasons remain, so very stagnant and overwhelmed.

For not that torment, _it cuts inside_ and removes all hope.
She was once all of my life, but as of today we are both now ghosts.
But I do wish to stay, and I would maybe then find some greater lesson.
As then and now, seeping deeper, into the burning hell fires.

As our God can't save us, it is all left up to faith.
Hope of some better morning, as tomorrow is erased away.
It feels so damn cold, as she gropes my heart, there burning in hell.
It is as of now that we must say, "_not-then holds the true meaning of our doubts._"

The Shattered Planet

Our world is ending, so maybe this is it.
My mind is breaking, as I cut off my own skin.
To prove to you, that I am just that sick and twisted.
Our world is ending, so we need to only smile.

So come laugh with me at the end of the rope.
Please just say, that which I believe I already know.
Let us take that chance, and end this fucked up world of pain.
Come help me pull the trigger, as I step away.

My love I do believe I'm back now, and ready to take control.
I am just only a shell, but maybe this time the pieces might hold.
We are so very great, here as our tormented world comes to an end.
So let us escape this shattered planet, and find love once again.

"For onward moves the sands of time, into that yet to be..."

Illustrated Murders

Can you not see upon the lips of tragedy?
Taken to that place where all our secrets hide.
Then into the twisted, thought of that grave.
Has been spoken over, and still it ends the same.
Of a darkness that this soul wishes to no longer endure.
A fucked up notion which stands today as but a pointless bore.
For as of then, that moment when we had reached the light.
Only to find that truly we had gone blind.
"GOD HELP ME PLEASE TO FORGET THAT DAY!"
All of those hidden whispers, lain so gently into my ear.
Then as my fragile soul was raped, and my mind left in fear.
There is but now that conflict, eating me so beautifully insane.
For I *shan't ever know* the bliss of that which cannot be.
As then left to only bleed out, all the fragmented memories of then.
Still I can't forgive myself for my unending immortal sins.
It is brilliantly drawn, in chalk lain there in the back room...
Oh fear not that sadistic moment, forgotten deep in the past.
Can you not see the truth upon the lips of that illustrated murder?
Held there in the open thought of all fact, and sadly is such.
Left to be only behind the page, cradled upon our thoughts of sanity.

A Candlewick Burnt

A candlewick burnt, and then this mind flooded deep with wax.
As for hours upon hours of digging, into the middle of the soft wrist.
It's taken then to that fact of naught, raped, beaten, shattered and lost.
So we scream for decades passed, still all the agony refuses to pass.
Please wake me there, at the true death of our mortal pride.
Place the last fragment of that memory, there behind the child's eyes.
And speak clearly of that one remaining chance for hope.
But still it cannot change the fact of this broken and tattered soul.
With a candlewick burnt, and then all light rushed out of this mind.
Forever into darkness shall we stay lost, *eternally wandering through time.*
It is that notion, of our futile attempt at trying to say that we can love.
It truly is dark here, within this soul that shall always be crushed.
Beaten, bruised, bleeding and dead, *and still the wax is warm in my hands.*
Red, it is bleeding out and soon shall we know that we lost our chance.
A candlewick burnt, life is gone, and we welcome death.

So Feel Me There

Feel me there, at the reconnection of this twisted line.
Push it deep until it bleeds, and let us laugh as we go blind
For what the fuck! And the truth is that we are at the end.
Please take me there, erase all care, and truly I am alone.

Break that answer at the tip of the smoldering blade.
Separate the flesh, to know that it is all the same.
Push God back in the reasons, to know who we truly are.
Left there waiting at the end, for all of this to start.

Please hate me now, for I am that demon from hell.
Love me now, then watch as all of what we are is gone.
For nothing to be yet always to bleed, away the knowledge of it.
So feel me there, without a care, to know the truth.
"We are now at the end..."

No In-Between

Scream for me now, then watch as the boiling steam leaves.
So very cold within, but this might be a dream.
With troubles constant building, bringing forth that notion.
For this is the perfect moment to prove, "I truly am dead."

Of not that torment, which drives its way into my pain filled head.
This is that meaning, it makes so much sense here at this time.
And now that I come to think of it, *all of those years I must have been blind.*
For now I can see, the hourglass broken and we're running out of time.

Please scream for me now, then weep as you know it will not help.
Come visit me someday, here within the abysses of hell.
Now just take from me, all that could have ever meant a thing to her.
Then as the switch is thrown, we wish to but only learn.

There is no in between, it is at this moment, for all or naught.
There is no chance for me, now I realize my soul is lost.
There is no time to waste, the end now upon our lips.
There is but no hope left, hidden in-between the jagged stitch.
"And all is a miss, upon that final kiss, so my love goodbye."

"I Said I Would Laugh."

I said I would laugh, as the atom bombs fell.
I said I would save you, but was too overwhelmed.
I said that I would love you, until the very end of time.
I said that I'm sorry, but still the sorrow remains in mind.

You said that you would be there, to catch me as I fell.
I have fallen for ages, and have still yet to reach an end.
I want my heart to stop now, it is rusted and full of tar.
You said that you would be there, to save me from the dark.

I said that I would hold on, if it meant that I could keep you.
I said that we would be forever, that one single fact of the word.
I said that I would be there to protect you, yet it was you I hurt.
I said that I would laugh, when our world comes to an end.
"We are all laughing now, so turn the page..."

FUCKED TO DEATH

She always remembered every lustful touch.
She was there to keep me down, and forever emotionally fucked.
She was the greatest of the worst things I ever had in my life.
So very disappointing to know just how easily these *papers will burn*.
And Oh so Goddamn funny that we still will never learn.

She would stand there above me, blood rushing off the blade.
She would taste it, then look me in the eyes and tell me that *I am* insane.
She would ride me, so very deep into the dirt and beyond my rage.
It's just so funny that no matter what I try to say.
All of this eternal torment shall *Forever & Always* remain the same.

She always remembered where to place it, *so very hidden behind the rhyme*.
She knew just what to say then, *that it was so very awesome indeed*.
We took a chance back then, *to try our best to reach the stars*.
We have fallen for decades now, *here drowning within this shallow heart*.
I wish only to wake up now to see, *as my "fate" is still fucking me...*

I knew what to say back then, *when the line wasn't crossed*.
I remember how it felt to me, *constant smashing against my skull*.
I did love the fact, *that we were both screaming together in hell*.
I can still feel the touch, *of our once eternal despair*.
Lost within the moment, *now forever gone and "I don't know where."*

She was the greatest of the worst things that I ever had in my life.
Love so true, but then buried deep and forever under the ice.
She was there to remind me that I am just an insignificant waste.
She was always the one to tell me, that *"I"* was her one greatest mistake.
But she did fuck me to death, *"for now and always alone in our graves..."*

Sanity Is...

Sanity is... forgotten and left astray.
My soul it is... burning alone in hell today.
My "love" it is... dying here within my shattered heart.
My dream it is... lost now and never to regain.
Sanity is... so Goddamn very insane.
My thoughts they are... evil and will sadly never change.
Sanity it is... all I wish to hold today.
The truth it is...

The Blade In Me

For as it bleeds and fades away.
Flesh was lost and so was pain.
For lives left hanging over the edge.
Then all at once we smile in the face of death.

As ages were bleeding away any hope.
Then I whisper gently to that once forgotten ghost.
I was so sorry then, as I now am today.
So please take me there, "away from care," to let it just all drift away.

Come place the blade in me.
Twist it to bleed me dry and leave me lost.
At the dawn of that new chance at faith.
And again for miles upon miles of fighting through the frost.

It was once the truth that stood to keep the lines.
All is a miss and left so sick and behind the cries.
So you are the one that states that you've wept for me.
Now as the blade is pulled out, I have only to bleed.
"Away this life I do not deserve."

Locked & Grim

Fuck this pain that stands here dancing around in my head.
I hate this world, I do wish it all dead.
So take me God and put me back where I should be.
In hell with all other demons.
For that is the fate that I have chosen for me.

Locked so grim and I can feel the monster rising.
The anger is steaming, my soul now fleeting.
So scream with me, and let us watch as all hope dies.
Please say that you remember, that we have forgotten the truthful lie.

I do need this now, to just step over and enjoy the fall.
Smile my love, as all hope is lost.
Here deep in the hell which you try to say is but my *own sick world*.
Locked and grim, fueled by only hate, "and I never did learn..."

Bloodstained Weeping

Maybe now, the Devil has a better hold on me.
Still I wish my soul to be forsaken, for all the bloodstained weeping.
Over those paper sheets and photos of loves left in the past.
Maybe I can just let go now, and burn until I am only ash.

God can you reach my sanity, to tell me that I in fact am insane?
The murderer of an innocent soul, I left it there in that frozen grave.
For my heart it is dead, but still it is waiting to die.
Blood drops running down the sides of our faces, for we have no tears left to cry.

And oh yes this is me, the poet that had sold his once beautiful soul.
To be forever here in darkness, so very damned and so very cold.
For there must have been a reason, some direction to the chaos.
I do wish to not be forgiven, for all of our bloodstained weeping...

"Please forget me here, for now and always."

To Reach the Heavens

Then reaching deep into the platinum skies.
As the last echoing memory fades behind these eyes.
For words unspoken yet felt so gentle in this heart.
Reaching far beyond the golden clouds and into the forever.

To touch her face, all that was sadly left buried in the past.
To know now what it means, to never end the stress.
As once was so much greater, in a time of not this moment.
What then is there to hold onto I say, but only the constant wonder.

Then reaching deep into the cold abyss of space.
As all alone out here, drifting deeper and deeper into the unknown.
For all of those kisses that left a scar here upon these lips.
Still venturing deeper, but never to be missed.

As then set to be the norm, of this twisted and tattered soul.
Hopes upon endless hopes that all my loves may find pure grace.
For then to know the outcome, here lost so deep in space.
Hoping to reach the heavens, so my soul may someday find rest...

Let's Trip the Lines

Let's trip the lines of both beauty and grace.
Then we shall dissect that creature of pure honor and faith.
To taste the pleasure of the grim dripping deep within the shallow.
Upon the notion that was never brought to light...

Let's trip the lines of horror and the fact of what I was.
Let's destroy the chatter of the funny little demons inside my lungs.
Upon that twisted thought dancing upon the noon, and lovely smiles.
So come then with me my love and let us trip deep unto another mile.

Let's trip the lines of sanity and the God that made us real.
Let's say that we want absolution as we tend to those wounds that can never heal.
Then it pushes so much deeper and far passed the point of no return.
Let's trip all the lines of faith and see what it is that we have learned...

Felt Putrid Hearts

I find myself out here, drifting alone in the middle of an endless ocean.
The sky so dark and black, as if all the stars in the heavens had died.
I find myself out here alone, drowning and no one can save me...
For it is at this moment that all my nightmares now return to haunt me.

For I cannot escape it, the sad and grim facts of my tattered past.
For it is I that truly tried to save this, world from ending in horror and death.
I said that I loved you, but only to watch you burn, and nothing remains but ash.
I did say that I would always be with you, so I hid you deep within my chest...

It all was such an awkward movement, as beginning to step over the ledge.
Then for miles I fell, and awoke drifting alone here upon this ocean of death.
"It meant so much to you," when I wasn't there to fight all the pains away.
For I have failed you my love, and now I shall be marked forever damned.

To be so weak and pathetic, "I do always seem to fuck it up in the end."
I did once say that I loved you, but that story ends the same again.
But no - God cannot deny me, of the bliss of knowing that I truly have won.
As you are still loved and felt to be forever - within my putrid heart.
"I shall never let go..."

Ten Million Into the Dirt

Fade me gone, into the last chance of gaining hope.
Beat me down, and I am not the man you thought I'd be.
Respect now the demeanor, then forced into a tragic lock.
Ten million lost at this battle, and this war is far from done.

It feels so wrong, to laugh as watching you scream for release.
Then tomorrow comes, and yesterday wishes but to remain.
As all of the toxic poisons, bleed out of this twisted mind.
Swallow now and smile, for it will all be fine...

Fade me gone, into the last hour and then all goes blank.
I wish to fight the inevitable, but death won't give me a chance.
I do need to stop this, all of the constant tripping through the unknown.
I too do wish to cut and bleed, away any knowledge of then...

Into the dirt falls any remote chance, of ever finding grace.
Within our earth, hidden there in plain sight where all can see.
Into the dirt, goes ten million more statistics that once had names.
Within our earth, we lie hidden, in plain sight – for all to see...

For We

For we are the voices, whispering into your heart.
We are the madness that makes you "Unique."
We have been with you all along, "inside".
We are the hidden truth found in your every dream.

For God took notice, upon the decay of his word.
We all knew what it meant, although so absurd.
We tried our best to answer the Devil's questions.
We now are screaming for you to open your eyes and awake!

For we have been there always.
Speaking the insane truth that your heart has dearly feared.
We hold all the meanings, as to what it is that lurks inside.
For we are the only, truth of God, he did ever need...

On Scope

Oh dear God, what now has - become of me?
For I fear I am lost, waking here - in an eternal dream.
For that *not-said*, left behind at death - where hope could sadly *not-reach*.
It is as it was meant to be, felt both bitter and sweet - then taken back once again...

Oh dear Satan, what now has - become of me?
On scope the logic, *mixed with nonsense* - laughing as the angels weep.
For that *not-said*, turning to rage once again – I need this to get me by.
So farewell to all, *for now all is lost* - and it is time to find some sleep...

Acid Set-Forth Bliss

Acid set forth bliss my love, *"Can you taste the sweetness in the air?"*
Burning stones fall from the sky my love, *"This just might be the end!"*
The face on the clock said it was time, *"Now here comes a little death."*
Acid set forth bliss my love, *"Can you not taste the neon raindrops?"*

I feel like I'm a monster now, waiting for my chance to feast.
I remember only fragments of whom and what I am, such an innocent creature.
I know that I am trying to, but it wasn't ever my choice to take that step.
Come then with the answers my dear, and let us escape beyond the sky.

Acid set forth bliss my love, *"Can't you feel the awesome sounds of laughter?"*
Again I cut and come undone, *"Now take then the power and let not-it flex!"*
We must face the fact of what we've done, *"Fuck it all, again and again!"*
Acid set forth bliss my love, *"But can't you not taste the sound of weeping?"*

I believe that I am the Devil now, or maybe just a human.
I think the water has risen, but I can't seem to drown.
I know that I am happy, so insanely happy to know I've failed.
Acid set forth bliss my love, but we are dead now – and it's all the same...

Chapter 2

Passed the Past...

<u>Militant</u>

Esoteric influences resonating within the miseries of our past.
As all to be but standing there behind that open door.
Just screaming! Just weeping! Just Dying! And still hoping for *Release.*
Taken then to another level, of this damned eternal - *metaphoric maze.*

So come then and push that bullet right through my head.
Rip out all of the demonic memories, of this sick demented mind.
Rape my soul my love, once again, for it is dead and so am I.
Fuck all of your pity, upon *"you"* I shall not waste my time...

Obscure voices trying to escape the other side of reality.
They are all left now as a subliminal message upon the wind.
It screams in anger! It screams in pain! It wants to love but never again!
So just take from that, the fact of our dying hopes of ever to be.

So come then and cut me open and take out all within.
Burn my corpse and erase all the evil words that I have said.
"For I am that demon, which you've feared all of your pathetic life."
But still I have to say "Fuck it" and I know that I am right...

<u>Radical Realities</u>

Disconnected from the hive, with radical realities tormenting this mind.
It falls twisted and crying, for it knows not its true nature.
For I am that monster whom has no face, "the visionary with no faith."
As forward falling behind the silver lining, where God cannot see.

For that of my insane motives, driving the wrath into the light.
Feasting upon human flesh, for I am that much of a freak!
The forgotten and beaten child, left weeping alone *where no one can see.*
Disconnected from this mind, as the radical realities eat me alive.

Left up to the point of, it's breaking against the edge.
Please hold onto me my love, as we fall away once again.
Damn all of this nonsense, that *holds me true* to the fact of what's inside.
Upon the endless radical realities, dissolving within my mind...

"As I watch you my love – simply fade away..."

BoneBreak

Life left fleeting upon death eternal.
As we had kissed the lips of God and hoped it to last.
It has all but gone away as hope was failing.
The bones were then broken and won't ever grow back.

For death begets life.
As pleasure begets pain.
So I continue to kill my brain cells.
Just to keep me sane...

With spoken truths lied the hidden meanings.
There standing at the end looking back.
Then as she said that it was all over.
I had opened my eyes to watch it all begin.

With life left fleeting upon our deaths eternal.
We missed our chance to regain a fragment of our past.
With love left blinded as all our hopes were failing.
All the bones have been broken and can't ever grow back.

Thrusting & Screeching!

Speak then and give it to me.
The motive of the murder, there as the angels weep.
For I am that bastard in whom you've always hated.
"Please forgive me for not being what you wanted."

As there you go just kicking and screaming!
PUT YOUR HANDS DOWN RIGHT FUCKING NOW!
I SWEAR TO GOD THAT I AM GOING TO KILL YOU!
And once again I know that I am indeed just that *mad...*

I tried my best to never hurt you.
Yet in the end I feel so great to know that I did.
For I have always hated that weakness.
It waits in your heart and makes me so damn sick.

GOD I SWEAR THAT I AM GOING TO KILL YOU!!!
YOU FUCKING LITTLE WATSE OF TEARS AND LIFE!
I DO INDEED WANT TO MURDER, ALL OF WHAT YOU ARE!
Again I've lost track of the meanings, *as you thrust, screech and fucking die.*

Lucent

Was taken and hated, *beat down* while screaming.
Was lost there standing at the *wake* of the dying hopes held for naught.
I'd love this to be the undeniable truth but sadly it is not.
We have gone now to a limbo, left somewhere lost in space.
And beyond any chance of again, it just might be alright.
"Yes I know you can see right through me."
For I am the nonsense, I am that bastard, "*Just a fucking waste of time!*"
It was a grand thought once, but then it burned away.
You were my love once, as of now but only a maggot filled grave...
I am a demon, standing right behind the mirror.
"Yes I know you cannot see me, *but trust me - I'm right here.*"
Maybe I'm just a ghost, a phantom lost between.
For once again it begins to happen, *we cannot deny the nature of the beast.*
So I'd love to say that this is it and all was as a dream.
But that is not the case, and now the rage – it grows.
For I am right here with you, hiding within your broken soul...

As I Strangle You...

As I strangle you, I get so excited.
Watching you kick and gasp for air.
But your life at that point is in my hands.
Goddamn I do love it, to feel your heart race.
As I strangle you, I love to hear you gasp.
With that hopeless thought that there might be a chance.

As you are dying, I feel my blood begin to rush.
And there is something there, twisting in the back of my mind.
It twists and twists until there comes a snap!
You are dead now my love and I can only laugh.
Only laugh... only laugh... only laugh...
Laugh... laugh... laugh...
Laugh...

The Guinea-Pig

So there hides the questions, of what was left behind.
There stands all the motives, from this so very twisted mind.
For there we are screaming, as our flesh is torn away.
Please awake my love – my world, or we shall never be saved.

Come now and follow me, into the answers of this damned war.
Love me for I do love you, as once upon a time, and I do hope more.
For that to reach to highest, point of the fact that all is but lost.
We are so very cold now, frozen in time and never to defrost.

So I scream, weeping as I watch my whole world come to an end.
But I was happy once, yet now I can only hold onto all our sins.
For I was a monster, the freak that laughed as they all fell.
I am the guinea-pig, the test-subject that learned the truth...

So there hides all the questions, of an answer overlooked.
Here we are now, ready to step over the ledge and smile.
So please awake now my love, for I am right here at your side.
Oh please kill all memories of me my love, then open your eyes.
"Smile and walk away..."

It Then Snaps!

Let us forget the meanings.
Let us dive in and remain below the waves.
For can you speak it now correctly.
Can you see what is waiting for you below the grave?
So come now and love it.
Come now and burn me.
Turn your head away as I scream with a laugh.
For all of what was is forgotten.
It was taken away and won't ever come back...
Just let us fall now so much deeper into the haze.
It then snaps and I weep as I'm realizing that I am insane.
Please go now and save us!
Save us from ever becoming but a forgotten page.
Please my love.... Just walk away...
Walk away...

Weak & Worthless

Smiles as here I plummet, for ages *just falling* from the stars.
I think that I might be high now... as the fear it washes away.
I want to hold you, so close in my arms and to know that we are safe.
Please just reach out to me my love, take my hand and let us escape.

There it's found now, *within these bones in which your hatred still breaks.*
All is misplaced, or have I awakened within a once forgotten dream.
I am so *weak & worthless*, but soon enough I shall be erased.
There I fall again now, falling eternally through time and space.

We've fought this war for ages, only to learn that we shall never win.
We've killed them all, and now we bathe in the acid, blood and sins.
Please say only, that the Devil knows that we are home.
Please tell me – God, that this is all just a fucked up dream...

With smiles as here I plummet, still falling from the stars.
Trying to reach out, but I am sadly never going to grasp.
I am so fucking *weak & worthless*, no better than putrid trash.
Please just reach out to me my love, take my hand, *and let us escape.*

Bastard By Nature

Poetic words unspoken, now forgotten with time.
As for so many years, here digging deep behind these dying eyes.
To see what it was, that birthed such a demonic being.
As I stare back into the mirror, it is our broken past my heart does seek.

Still I try to reach it, still I want to believe it.
That someday God shall return and I might be saved.
But then again I remember, the fact of what lies inside.
I am a bastard by nature, a dead soul remembering life.

With poetic thoughts decaying, here within all that could be.
"Oh please," I just want to smile and let this all free.
To see what could become of this dark twisted mind.
I want to be dead and forgotten, *just to separate myself from these times.*

"In death - they shall discover the truth..."

Her

It falls in deeper and she speaks to me no more.
I was but a waste of her time, just a useless bore.
We had said that we would hold on until time came to an end.
Time is dead my love, as are we – for once again...

It breaks back further and she wishes that I would just up and die.
I am that nonentity, just a mother-fucking waste of a poetic mind.
As now to be and then set free, as she places my ashes under her scars.
As then to know, and the blood it flows, for we are sadly torn apart.

It was a chance we took, a great long-shot indeed.
As then to feel that inevitable push back and break-down.
It was I that was but only a waste of time, just a mother fucking bore.
For it was her that had said to me, "Our love is dead, forever more..."

Faces Below the Waves

So all is now tearing at the seams.
I had awoke to my death and found that life was but a dream.
It was the pain that had made it, feel as if I was at one point real.
As now it is unavoidably true, "there is no saving me."

As then the wax it cools, thickens, and covers all of this being.
There is only blood now, here on my hands and it tastes so sweet.
As then shall they come to know, of what lies there below the waves.
All of our memories go, and we all just burn away.

As taken so very far from faith, to where the Devil feels at home.
I was once a great love in your life, but now a shattered stone.
Yet I know that I can reach it, the switch that holds our true ends.
But then the rain it comes, but it can't wash us clean of our sins.

So please just take me to the ocean and let me drift below.
And I shall remain right here, with all the other unknown faces below the waves.
I kind of feel as if at one point, I might have had a soul.
It is cold down here, below the waves where I shall always remain...
"So very cold."

Earthworms Under Flesh

I can feel them, just beneath the surface of my flesh.
They are eating, me from the inside - to the out!
I think that I am dead now.
I am dead to you, and I cannot get out!

I want to fall here and remember.
Remember the fact that I was once loved by a Devil.
It is true my dear, and you cannot change it.
I'm sure that I am dead now my love, "I am dead and damn I love it...!"

I scream out loud and no one can hear it!
I cut and bleed out, a rotten bloody tar...
As then the smoke it invades us, to show what could have been.
Like the time when I last held you, "I know that this is it...!"

So come with hate and **FUCK** me!
Yes I am nothing more than your dirty little whore.
Please try your best to change this, as they are eating me alive.
Oh yes I am dead my dear, dead to this world in which I despise.

The earthworms are crawling, through all of my hollow veins.
They made their way into my head and have now replaced my brain.
Oh FUCK all of this tormenting bullshit, infesting right under my flesh!
Just let me fall, and then fill this empty grave...
Forget me my love, "For yes I am dead..."

Passionate Particulars

She was walking to that place where she hides the truth of our story untold.
She was weeping all the way, alone and so very damn cold.
She was whispering to herself, of a fact that our hearts still wish to deny.
She was fighting her way to get there, so far beyond the other side.

She was hiding a fact, there with her troubled thoughts and heart.
She wanted me, to be erased for all time and forever more.
She was weeping because of a fear that has sadly only grown with time.
She still regrets that she had ever loved me, so she only wishes for the other side.
"For there she may someday find peace."

Impulsive

As still the torment is growing, my soul is soon to break.
For once I did indeed feel love, but now it is gone away.
I am damned and nothing more than a sick creature of the past.
I am the hatred that is growing, here within my own demented head!

*I can't **FUCKING** take it! All I have ever loved is now dead.*
I can't feel like I'm alive anymore, here in someone else's head!
Please let me go now, so I can find that place where my soul shall forever lie.
*Just **FUCKING** cut my throat now! So I can let go here and die.*

For not of any better motives, only sorrow, only shame.
Mother take me back to hell now, for I know that's where I deserve to be.
*I'm not the **FUCKING** good guy, I am not the hero of this story.*
I am but the ink that fills this once forgotten page...

I want now to let go, and then fall away into one of my dreams.
To watch as another demon rises, and takes it's hold of me.
***I AM A FUCKING MONSTER!** I am but a child that wants to go home.*
I am weeping at your feet now, here with my broken soul.

So is it so very impulsive, to reach beyond and kiss the lips of God?
"And while I'm here, I might as well use some tongue..."
As Oh to be and then set free, all of the miseries of my now forgotten past.
Please just let me be – to fade away, so you my love can but only laugh...

Attain My Sympathies

Hold onto the madness as the teeth push through the flesh.
Like a madman that wants an answer, "Someone better fucking guess!"
To attain my sympathies, for the truth is that I do no longer care.
Only smiles remain, as time washes all, of our beautiful world away.
Oh it tastes like heroin, as it bleeds out of my shattered eyes.
Like the Devil as he calls to me, has forgotten that I'm not alive.
Of just a memory, still lingering on for a reason unknown and lost.
It truly is insane, to think that sanity had ever mattered at all.
Like the dead that are waiting, for their purgatory to come to an end.
You must attain my sympathies, if we are ever to awake again.
"Beyond tomorrow..."

As the Stone Bleeds

As the stone bleeds it speaks my name.
And I can't find anybody, to tell me where I stand today.
So maybe I'm just dreaming of this strange familiar place.
Where pain is God - and we are all dead.

Can please we take the next step?
Then as we fall, the rope tightens and we swing about.
It's like a jagged memory of so long ago.
It's like I opened my eyes, then I went blind.
So I listen to you laugh as you let me go...

As the stone bleeds, it reminds me of my shames.
All of the facts that I've been hiding, there in her grave.
For I want only to reach out and tell you how I do feel.
But I realize now that I am alone, all alone on-top this hill.
"With sanity dying – forever in me..."

Feeding You - To Yourself

Come then and let's see what calms the shakes.
Let us watch our selves as we come undone, all over again.
Let's try to say "*We mattered!*" right before they turn off the lights.
We never did truly matter, so fuck it all, "*Let's just say goodbye.*"
To end some torment, all of the nonsense that we've endured.
So again we speak of that rage, in which we hide behind that open door.
Cannot these voices stop screaming in me? It's driving me insane!
For what is it that keeps us going, so far over the edge!?
I think that now it's bleeding, from that gaping wound in its chest.
It might be dying, just fighting to end all of the horrific pain.
Then we realize that it is both me and you, here bleeding so insane!
And there I go now, feeding you to yourself.
And I laugh, and I laugh, so very deep here in hell.
With smiles all around, such sick and distorted faces.
They are weeping, they are screaming, and I know it's all in my head!
I think I'm dying, I think I'm frying, yes it just might be...
So far passed any form of logic, as I am feeding you to - yourself.
Laughing as I know that I am feeding myself to - me...

43

Regurgitating Bloody-Tar

Here it comes now, fuck it's starting to burn.
We tried to say that we'll hold on.
But then the hour came and all did fail.
I want to just release and fade away now.
Just to once again be at her side...

Damn it, here it goes again! And I can't hold it back!
I'm trying my best to hold on.
Even now, so far beyond death.
And there it goes now, the regurgitations of bloody tar.
It steams as it spreads all over the table and onto the floor.

God please wake me! I know now that this is hell!
I want to be with her again, to keep my heart so calm.
The answer it is showing now, within the tar of my dead lungs.
I need to just get out, and stop killing myself of the fact.
That we are all dead now, and can't ever come back...

Against Religion

It is a notion that we've gone over, for so very many years.
It was a prayer from the heart, now just lonely frozen tears.
As God it waiting, and hoping that we make the right decision.
Our world is dead now, as here I stand against religion.

Please save us God, for we know naught what is it is that we have done.
We are all but ignorant children, wielding a loaded gun.
We did try our best, to save this damned world of the weak.
But no man can ever win at this war, "God we need to be saved."

It was an option, to just let it all play out and find that answer.
But we did kill all hope for our souls to ever be saved.
As God is dead now, *and it was us that killed him when we made our decision.*
For we are all dead now, and forever I'll stand against your religions.

"God save us..."

Hostilities of War

It falls great upon the doorsteps, of the sanctuary of peace.
It's left shattered and disgusting, cringing in rage.
I want more of an answer, something standing stronger than this.
We cannot do this any longer, it's time we release some stress.
But at some point it might get better, but oh not today.
The war is almost over, but again it ends the same.
Death is constant growing, and this fact will never change.

Now it's time we make a stand, then laugh as we all fall.
Because I don't think there would be a greater irony at all.
So it gets us through these blood soaked years.
As we are still fighting away all the cold and lonely tears.
I need to just let go, and admit that I cannot save us now.
It is time for me to accept, the truth of my pathetic life.
It is at this point that we must, end the hostilities of war...

"We must stop the bloodshed."

Passion As We Suffer

Passion as we suffer, memories lost over time.
A gun that is loaded, and it is about that time.
Answers softly whispered, echoing within our dreams.
Felt agony upon the pleasures, hidden where none can see.

Anger as we remember, that soon we are to forget.
Life once held a meaning, but now it is all amiss.
We had once known the truth of, all hidden inside.
We died to achieve the power, but that was only a lie.

Passion as we suffer, tormented for all of our mistakes.
Damnation and we are weeping, alone in hell – ashamed.
But it makes sense, that all we've ever loved is presently dead.
With passion as we suffer, forgotten now once again.

Left Under the Fault

Again it's tearing, and no one's caring.
I wish that God would take me away.
Again I'm burning, and there is no learning.
So, why the fuck am I still insane?
As again it's cutting beyond the torment.
For yes I am still so twistedly whore-bent.
There is no chance now, to save this moment.
Now all is dead, and so beautifully silent.

We've tried to reach it, the higher level.
We fell so deep, into the hells fire.
There was a chance once, for us to preserve that feeling.
But love is dead now, and we cannot save it.
Yet at least I'm trying, still weeping and dying.
I just wish that God would take me away.
So far beyond this twisted moment.
In which it's my fault, that we are all insane.

This Is An Awkward Sight.

It is so awkward, yes indeed.
As watching all these angels stabbing me.
Of course I am a demon, but what the hell?
It was God that had laughed, as he watched me fail.

I want mother to wake me, from this pointless dream.
I want death to just take me, "*he mocks as I scream.*"
This world it truly hates me, the damned soul that had tried.
I want someone to just wake me, and tell me I have died.

It is so awkward, yes indeed.
As I'm watching myself, killing me.
Of course I am a poet, tormented with nothing to say.
This is an awkward sight.
Watching God laugh, as he throws me away...

Until It Stops Weeping

Lost track of time.
Why can't it stop weeping?
We stepped over the line.
The blade, it cuts us deeply.
Lost forever, for we are blind.
Why can't it stop weeping?
I want to step over that ledge.
Fall away, as life is fleeting.
Our dreams they are burnt away.
So we all hide them discretely.
I want to know who is in that grave.
The lost soul forever dreaming.
But for now, I must step away.
And admit that I have no feelings.
I lost track of time again today.
For some reason it just can't stop weeping.
For the blade it is left in, so very deeply.
I want to say, that we'll be okay.
But that can never be true.
Until it stops weeping.
All of the ghosts remember now.
Of the life that was fleeting.
It is time for us to let it go.
But it will never truly end.
Until it stops weeping.

The Child Of Misery

Left here ignored, the child of misery.
Body parts hidden under the floor.
But it means not what you think.
Our Devil will never have control.
Of this child of misery.
I know at times, I sound so cold.
But that's the way, it will always be.
For I know that there is no chance, to save this soul.
Yet that is the life, I had chosen for me...

HATE ME MY LOVE!?

Falling once again, into my pit of despair.
Through clouds of LSD, swimming through her hair.
I fall in deeper, but all by choice.
Hate me my love, and lock away this void.

I want not to be remembered, for being a demon from hell.
Yet I know that it is true, I did try and I did fail.
So hate me now my love, just fucking throw me away.
Erase me my love, and then burn this tattered page.

As falling once again, into my pit of despair.
Drinking down the LSD, with all the smoke and purple tears.
Please pull the trigger, and then just walk away.
Hate me my love, oh please just throw me away.

StillBorn

Fuck – such a tragedy.
Lusts and insanity.
With bloody fingertips, digging the grave.

Death takes a hold of me.
Something is wrong with me.
Weeping blood as I dig this grave.

The snow, it is falling now.
Tears of blood, they are gushing out.
Here at the bottom of this hollow grave.

At some point, God must answer me.
As the Devil weeps – oh such a tragedy.
As alone I wait here, in this cold grave...

As Judgment Is Pressed

As my judgment is pressed, I truly don't know where the fuck I am.
Maybe I'm at that place, between dreams and reality.
As again I rant on, about the death of my sanity.
But the truth is, that I wish all of the voices would just go away.

I am a damned soul, and will always be.
But truly I do not know, "where the fuck is this place."
Maybe in some way, I should never know.
The truth of what it is, waiting there all alone.

As my judgment it pressed, I am ready for inevitability.
As I release my last breath, *I begin to wonder where eternity is taking me.*
Maybe out somewhere, a paradise of peace.
But the truth is, that I am burning now.
And I knew that's what would come to be.

"Mangled & Distorted."

My faith is broken, mangled and distorted.
It's time to end all of this panic and disorder.
We need just to breathe in.
Then maybe we will be okay.

We cannot deny that fate has spoken.
And we are all damned to reap that which we have sewn.
The price of peace, we could never afford it.
Our fates are now, so mangled and distorted.

Maybe on some level, we knew this would happen.
Maybe I could hear the thoughts in my head.
If all the voices would just stop fucking laughing.
But soon enough *they will* go away.

For our world is now broken and shattered.
Our hearts they are, all torn and raped.
Our souls remain mangled and distorted.
But it is our faith, in which needs to be saved.

Chapter 3

A Forward Step Backwards

Authoritative

"Listen now to what I say."
For soon it shall all be lost and within my grave.
Take note of all in which we have lived.
Remember my words as time erases them away.

"Do now as I have told you."
For soon enough only dust and ash shall remain.
Try to hold onto all that you have ever loved in life.
Remember what it is that I have said.
"As again I am, but thrown away..."

A Darkness Of the Truth

So bitter now, and was such a darkness of our youths.
It's not over yet, but God told me that the end was coming soon.
As we are dying today, listening to all of the angels as they weep.
For the truth is that our entire world was sadly taken away.

To a place where no soul can ever reach.
Beyond time and space, a place hidden within our dreams.
And we have tried to regain it, we did try and we did fail.
We wanted to hold on forever, *but forever came* and we're now in hell.

So very tormented, by none other then ourselves.
It is a darkness of the truth, still locked deep in hell.
Within a void that not even our God can reach.
Still screaming within our hearts, still dying within our dreams.

Useless Minds.

Useless minds and deadly rhymes.
I guess nothing has changed at all but me.
Hours of pains, lusting sanity so insane.
So maybe the truth is that I'm just a freak.
Still trying my best and losing my breath.
But only because, under the waves, no one can breathe.
"Such useless minds, deadly rhymes and it's all a greater part of me...

Off Guard

It caught me off guard, when she said that she was sorry.
Sorry for ever feeling love for a demon like me.
It caught me off guard, when she dug into my scars.
She told me that I was a fuck up and that "I will die alone."

So maybe in the end, that is what was meant to be.
I was always told that I was heartless and so very weak.
I did try my best to be the good guy, but I did fail.
I stand here so tormented still, burning alone in my own hell.

For upon what actions, did condemn me to this?
It caught me off guard, when she shoved the razor into my wrist.
To remind me that I am just a fuck up, a waste of tears and pain.
I am nothing but a useless poet, still screaming insane.

It caught me off guard, when she kissed me upon my lips.
She then whispered into my ears, that I'll never be missed.
She laughed as I was falling, into the abyss of my own mind.
It caught me off guard, when she said, to just give peace more time...

Was This a Dream?

Was this a dream or a perverse reality in which was truly fucked!?
At some point I hope that I find an answer.
As to why it is that I'm but a shell of a man, lost alone in space.
Please help me to reach it, that much better side of mourning.
Now I can no longer understand, *all of the sick-demented voices in my head.*
Upon another rant, and I know that you are laughing at me..!
It's kind of like *a secret murder,* in which still haunts our every dream.
So was any of this in life ever truly real, *or just another delusion of mine.?*
Was this a dream, or just another fucking waste of our time?
Is there anybody out there, which is willing to take my hand?
Please somebody wake me now, from my eternal dreams of this...
"Just please somebody save me from my nightmares once again."
" *Was this but a dream?*"

That's Why We Scream

That's why we scream – as taking a forward step backwards.
The knives they all weep – *delicious poisons* into my spine.
The questions have all gone – and might never come back.
The truth of why we die – hidden behind the eyes of *Death*...

It is hopeless, and I don't think it's about to change.
The rain it is falling, now it's melting us away.
We are burning, screaming for God to save the day.
But God no longer cares, for souls in which cannot be saved.

That's why we scream – as the sky falls from above.
The world it does weep – for it knows that it is coming to an end.
No questions have been answered – no turning back at all.
That is why we smile, *as watching the atom bombs fall*...

I Felt Nothing...

I felt nothing as she dug her fingernails into my spine.
I am nothing but a dying creature, screaming in rage.
She held all of my heart then, within her soft hands.
I felt nothing, as she laughed at me and threw my heart away.

I know it's true indeed, that this pain I do deserve.
I want to believe, that someday I might be saved.
But you and I both know, in my life peace has no chance.
She did at one point love me, but she did never look back.

I felt nothing, as I was brutally murdered on that day.
I am nothing, but a recollection of sorrow and pain.
She was my reason, to live on and seize the day.
I felt nothing, as I was burned away...

"I felt nothing."

So Very Great

Indeed it was so very great, to watch my flesh being torn away.
To see the eyes of the Devil as he was laughing at me.
As watching God torturing me, for all the remainder of our eternity.
It rings true upon that fact, and it was so very great.
When I had died and then let go, to awake within my hell today...

It truly was so very great, when our world it all came to an end.
It's like I had stepped out of myself for a brief moment, but only to see.
That hope had died and we all let go, now we all fall away.
It's so very great to know the truth, _that none of us shall ever be saved..._

Pull the Thorns Out

Pull the thorns out and lie them down in a row.
Let us speak of the moment, lost somewhere in time.
We hold still the meaning to the ending.
"I feel that I am back now at where this story began."

Pull the trigger now and smile while I fall.
And here in the darkness you shall find my love, "_not a damn thing at all._"
So take me back there, to a time when I was at peace.
The years when I was so very tormented, by that _Angel's_ beautiful face.

Let's pull the thorns out, and then watch as I just bleed.
Let's close that door now, so maybe I can get some sleep.
Please pull the thorns out of my side, from between the ribs.
Pull the thorns out, "Yes I know, soon all shall be clear..."

A Skull Now Broken

A skull now broken, bleeding under the moon.
Life is over, so very far passed noon.
It was a secret, and I won't ever tell.
A skull now broken, blood seeping into hell.
A death still remembered, and I shall hold it to the end.
A hope that is dead now, dancing upon the wind.
"_I shall never let go my love, of my memories of then..._"

She Gave Her Soul

With today came a cold, chill of death felt in me.
With life came a question, for which we still seek.
In death will come an answer, and we hope soon to reach.
In pain we do know, that pride is all that's left of me.

She gave her soul, when she had said that she loved me.
She gave her heart, when her tears were constantly flooding.
She gave up her dreams, because she wanted us to be free.
Truly she gave up her soul, for loving a demon like me.

With today comes a shadow of the past, and we can no longer hold on.
With rage follows death, and it is the very same as then.
In death we hide the answers, *to the questions in which were never asked.*
In pain we are moaning, and sanity won't ever come back.

She gave me a kiss, and it had scared me for decades.
She gave to me a notion, in which I still can't comprehend.
She gave up her freedoms, just to be here at my side.
She gave up her soul to love me, "*but that was all a lie...*"

Then Shoot Me!

Come on then and shoot me!
Come on now and let's end this page!
Come on now and kill me!
Come take my hand and we fly away...
FUCK YOU BITCH JUST SHOOT ME!
Come on my love and open your eyes!
Just come on and say that you are here now!
Tell me that you have always been at my side.
So please my love just shoot me.
For at that point everything will be alright.
So come on now and shoot me!
Then just turn off the lights...

Ready to Dance?

Are you ready now to dance about without a care?
Are you ready now to dream aloud, and admit that God's not there?
Are you ready now to just let go and laugh as we fall backwards?
Are you ready now to cut my throat and fill your glass with laughter?

We are screaming "yes" and still hoping that salvation will arrive.
We have loaded the gun, and now our target is in our sights.
I have no more chance of ever regaining my heart.
So tell me my love, are you ready to dance, *way up here above the stars?*

Alone On Mars

Here I am alone on Mars.
Come to think of it, I've gone too far.
But no matter what I do, still I can't escape this war.
So at this point I know, truly I will die alone.

So here I am alone on Mars.
Digging so very deep, but still to this day I find no heart.
But all will be okay, as I admit that I was thrown away.
And then was left alone out here, so tormented and in pain.

Here I am alone today.
And I don't think that it's ever gonna change.
So that's the hand that was dealt to me.
So now I wait alone out here, left to wander with only my pride.

So here I am alone again.
Left out here, and still waiting to depart.
I've wished for release, I've wish to be saved.
Yet still I'm alone on Mars.

"My dead planet, vast it stands as my grave."

You Still Feel It

You still feel it when I call your name.
The chill that runs up your spine and into your brain.
Oh do not deny me, for I am the monster you found within.
You still feel it as I call to you, from the other side of the mirror.

You are the nonsense, the broken logic within this shell.
You are the unforgiven, you are but the one who failed.
You still feel it, after so very many long years.
All of the pain, it still echoes inside.

You still hate me, for laughing at the world as it fell.
You want to kill me, for destroying all of your loves.
You want me to die now and to simply fade away.
I am but the monster found within you, and that can never change.

Press it Below the Flesh

Press it deep below the flesh.
Watch it scream and lose its breath.
It ends in torment, it ends in rage.
So somebody please get me out of this cage!

Cut it open and take out all of what was inside.
Tell me that you love me and then close your eyes.
And I laugh at the murder, I laugh – weeping in pain.
Take me back to that moment, when I was frozen under the rain.

Press it deep below the flesh.
Smile as the blood gushes from its chest.
It feels like pleasure, it tastes so strange.
So just try to remember, that we were never sane...

Tear into the heart now and tell me how it feels.
It's like we've done this before, it's such an awesome thrill.
And we laugh at the slaughter, we weep again all the same.
Press it deep below the flesh, tear it out and tell me how does it taste...

Soon To Taste the Burn

I am worthless, waiting for the last grain of sand in the hourglass to fall.
I am a ghost, and I will never be remembered at all.
I've gone through this life, just one battle after the next.
And soon to taste the burn, and here in hell I take my next step.

I've been reaching out, all of my sad and wretched life.
I have been cast out, and will never again see the light.
I have died again, for the millionth time.
And soon to know the truth, after we turn off the lights.

We have searched for so long indeed, for a God that is unfound.
We looked up to the heavens, and dug deep into the ground.
We have waited so long for an answer, as to why we are here.
And upon the endings shall arise the correct questions, in which we fear.

I am worthless, watching all the grains of sand fall from the hourglass.
And into the desert of eternal time and space.
I've gone once beyond this life and found what waits on the other side.
As we are soon to taste the burn, once we open our eyes...

As Naught to Be

As naught to be and then set free.
Left hidden below the golden sands.
As so soon to see what is to be.
And I hope someday they'll understand.

As naught to know and we just let go.
Then we fall away beyond reality and dreams.
To a better place where hope can thrive.
Left hidden behind, an Angel's eyes.

As naught to be and then set free.
Left to die as but a broken man.
As so soon shall we go and never are we to know.
The truth of what lies hidden below the golden sands.

In the Last Chance Of...

Maybe someday I will rise and save the day.
I wish that I was a hero, but I am treated as only a mistake.
Just a reluctant scapegoat, for the whole world to beat down.
Maybe I can save the day somehow, but that was just a dream.

I was a weak child, beaten down into the dirt.
I was a dreamer, and I guess that I never did learn.
But maybe someday I can reach it, the truths of my dismay.
Lost and left alone, in the last chance of ever being saved.

Maybe someday, I will grow and become a shooting star.
I wish that I could save us, from the pain of those scars.
I just need to remember, the truth that I am just weak.
I know I can never be the hero, but I still want to save the day...

I am just worthless, a waste of poetic tears and laughter.
I was a dreamer, but all this time I was awake.
If I try real hard, I might see something beyond all of this pain.
As I am bleeding here, in the last chance of...

It's Cutting

It's cutting deep into my eyes.
I'm sure that very soon I will go blind.
And there is no one to save me, no one to wake me.
There is no one here but the Devil and I.

It's cutting deep into my heart.
It's frozen now and made of tar.
And I'm sure that someday we will end some of this stress.
So I am hollow now, with nothing at all within my chest.

It's cutting in me, and I dare not say.
That of all I have ever loved and again taken away.
So that's my life, filled mostly with death.
So please place my dead heart, back into my chest.

They Came to Take Us.

The voices in my head, "*I think they're insane...*"
No matter what I do, I can't stop all of this pain.
O yes I am laughing, yes I am crying, I know what I am!
But they came to take us, to a room with padded walls.
They came to drug us, to keep us under control.
The voices and I are pissed now, and I won't take this shit!
The time for peace has passed now, so fuck it all, again *and* again!
They came to take us, to a nice and quiet place...

The little creatures in the back of my head, they are screaming.
All of the ghosts that I hide under my bed, I know they are dreaming.
We have been dreaming of the day, when all shall come to an end.
We want our lives back, and we won't say it again!
So give me that knife back, so I can open up your eyes.
They're trying to take us, to a place where we'll be left in the dark.
I can't stop all of my anger, it's too late for anyone to escape.
The demons have come to take us, deep into hell where we should stay.

Fuck Humanity!

Fuck Humanity, and all that it stands for.
With my broken sanity, I shall take control of this day.
Beyond any chance of, *that push* to the much greater side.
Fuck all of what we are today, so I guess that *we have* gone blind.

So can you see what it is that you have done?
Can you breathe, with the blade of the knife inside your lung?
Can ever we just end this, and smile as it will all be okay.
It's so damn funny that after all of this, we still have nothing to say.

So fuck all of humanity, and everything that it stands for.
I hate what we have become, nothing but a worthless bore.
I cannot just stand here and take it, I've gotta get the fuck out!
And again I know that I am stuck here, lost beyond the clouds.

So fuck humanity and all that it ever stood for.
Fuck our sanity, for it is driving me "*Goddamn insane!*"
Just take me away from all of this bullshit!
Shut it all up, and then fill my hollow grave...

Sweet Little Whispers

Still to this day, the voices are screaming within my brain!
It causes so much pain, and I feel as though I'm beginning to drown.
I want to escape this nightmare, but I never seem to awake.
And from my heart I can hear the sweet little whispers.
And they're telling me that I'm going to be okay.

My life it is in total chaos, and there is nothing that I can do.
Please my love, "come and save me, don't let me die alone..."
I want us to just leave this nightmare, *and feel the warmth of the suns rays.*
I can hear the sweet little whispers, echoing from within my heart.
Still they're telling me that I'm going to be okay.

My passions are all dead and faded, as is my dreams of any hope.
My life is it insane again, so I guess that nothing has changed at all.
My faith it is broken, as is *my once indestructible* heart.
Our world it has ended and nothing remains but dead space.
And on goes the echoes of the sweet little whispers.
Forever telling us that we are going to be okay...

We Go On Broken

We are beaten, we are bleeding.
Still we're crying, still alone and dying.
We are hated, so very hated for what we are.
We are broken, so beaten down and torn apart.

We are screaming, so painfully screaming.
We're still crying, forgotten and dying.
We are lost, so very lost and won't ever be saved.
We are broken, bloody weeping alone in our graves.

We are beaten, we are bleeding.
We are forgotten, lost and discarded.
We are hated, held down and then torn open.
We go on broken, still standing tall today...

Then Comes the Rain

Those words were spoken, and still so very little said.
The miles were walked, lost in someone else's head.
And upon a decade of remembering, what it is to feel pain.
Sorrow it fills this tormented heart and then comes the rain.

We are burning here, stuck in our own hell that we did make.
We are lost my love, or maybe just insane!
I can feel it tearing, into the back of my mind and into my thoughts.
I believe our world is flooding, and on it rains nonstop.

Death has come and spoken our names, and still it floods all the same.
The thoughts are all splintered, now but fragments of our past.
Of a time when we were happy, and had only to laugh away the pain.
A time when we had loved and lost, and then came the rain...

Note To Self:

Let's take a step back and try to get this straight.
Let's take the noose from around our neck.
"We'll have more time for that anyways."
Let's try our best to speak of it, that moment so "*Unknown.*"
Let's admit that we are forgotten, and nothing now but ghosts.

Let's pray to God then, and wait for him to reply.
We have turned into dust now, lost forever in time.
Let's just awake from this nonsense, and say that it was real.
Let's fall from the sky and laugh, as the ground draws near.
Let's just let it all go, then soon the answers will be clear.

Oh fuck it now, damn all of this bullshit to hell.
I can't take it anymore, so I'll make a note to self.
We are the dreamers, whom have never felt sleep.
We are the sleepers, which have never been awake.
We *can* save ourselves, from all of our futile mistakes.
We have to just let go, before it's too late...

Still Fighting To Breathe

Alone out here, stuck in space.
Still watching you, fading away.
I begin to question, if life was real.
And still I wish, for my wounds to heal.
As I'm left out here, all alone.
With only my sanity, to die in my soul.
And it is so hard to believe, that I'm left out here stuck in space.
Still fighting to breathe, as I watch you fade away.

Alone out here, stuck in space.
I do believe that I have forgotten, even my very own face.
"No" I just can't remember, what it is to be alive.
Now I'm out here in space, watching shooting stars just pass me by.
And still I wish, for all of this to just make sense.
I need not any forgiveness, I hold not any shame.
Though still I'm fighting to breathe, out here alone in space.
"And still I laugh, as I watch you fade away..."

Like Laughter & LSD

It tastes like *laughter & LSD* that fills this glass from which I drink.
And it seems so strange to watch you smile with no face.
"SO MAYBE I'M BEGINNING TO FREAK!!!!"
"MAYBE EXISTINCE WAS JUST A DREAM!!!!"
"BUT I DON'T FUCKING KNOW ANYMORE!!!!"
Yes it feels so smooth, when you rub your tongue upon my spine.
Then the rain it falls, like burning red neon lights.
And I begin to feel a slight flutter, all the demons in my mind.
I begin to question reality, and the fact that we are all blind.
Oh yes it tastes like laughter that waits at the bottom of this glass of LSD.
But maybe I'm just a memory, forgotten by God himself.
I do think that it's working *"GOD I THINK I'M GONNA DIE!!!!"*
I do feel a little better now *"THE DEMONS ARE EATING MY MIND!!!"*
But maybe I'm okay now "STILL DROWNING IN MY PAST!!!!"
It tasted like *laughter & LSD* that had once filled this empty glass...

The Master Of Despair

Here within this world of decay, I am the master of despair.
The truth of the matter, it still remains hidden in the clear.
And nothing I say could make the fact change.
For the time has come, and this world is mine.

All the cities on this earth are burning, and no one can be saved.
All the oceans have dried up, all the forests burnt away.
It was a perfect, forward step backwards, towards an absolution.
And into Armageddon we go, as upon our faces is only a smile.

Here within this broken world, of ash and decay, I am the master of despair.
As still beyond the riddle hides the shame, of never will we tell.
The time it has come, for all of us to step over the ledge.
Head first towards inevitability, and upon our faces is only a smile.

Of My Dead Loves

Ages upon ages of dead leaves filling my hollow grave.
Each turning into a single grain of sand.
And into the hourglass of time they are placed.
Echoing memories, of a life which was sadly thrown away.

And of all I cherish most, the memories of her smile.
I regret the most, of the moment when I had walked away.
It was an outcome in which I'd foreseen, and sadly it did come to pass.
Of all I had ever loved in life, it would have been her smile.

Then God and the Devil converse, over whom gets to keep my soul.
Then they both sadly remember, that I am but a shell of a creature.
A damned beast born of rage and sin.
Of all that I had said in my life, I remember only the laughter.

Chapter 4

Ending the World

If We All Let Go

If we all let go, then who would be left to say.
That it's been a great trip, falling a million miles below our graves.
And this world seems so strange, so demented here inside my head.
If we all let go, *we need then only to admit that we've always been dead.*

Forever lost in this frantic world, forgotten somewhere in time.
No flesh here remains, only these tattered bones and pointless cries.
For years still we are falling, here in my un-waking dreams.
If we all let go, then we could maybe awake somewhere at peace.

The torment is growing, and pleasure is felt all the same.
Nights upon nights of unending laughter, still echoing in my brain.
What of this poet still remains, but only hatred and anger?
If we all let go, then maybe we could find both peace and laughter.

These Bones Are Twisting

These bones are twisting like my mind.
The needles are sinking into my spine.
The Devil is laughing, and so am I.
Reality is forgotten, so let us just smile.

These drugs are delicious, they taste like laughter.
All the neon-lights are beautiful, winding like my soul.
My heart it is shifting, right out of place.
These bones they are twisting, as is this cold blade.

We are but a counterfeit, memory of our God.
And the truth shall remain hidden, forgotten but not lost.
The razors they are shifting, now bleeding me dry.
All of my bones are felt twisting, "I think I'm gonna die."

"So let us just smile..."

Cocaine & Murder

So much glory found at the edge of the blade.
Let us speak the truth that we shall never be saved.
Fuck all of the torment, revered as our faith.
Let's end this now, then burn all the evidence away.

I can still hear the screaming, into the long hours of the night.
I can still feel the pleasure, as the flesh separates.
The blood is everywhere, and the fresh human-meat tastes so great.
Magnificence upon the *cocaine & murder*, and then blown away.

Fuck all of the nonsense, leave only chaos and disorder.
Let us speak of the truth now, that God wishes not to save us.
It's so much of a pleasure, to know that their lives are mine.
It still tastes like *cocaine & murder,* forever plaguing this troubled mind.

"It's Coming..."

The end is coming and we won't even know.
Death has spoken and we all faded away.
Lives they are forsaken, demons controlling what we say.
The end it is coming, and we won't even know, "*we were taken away.*"

The monster is rising, he'll soon reach the surface.
We have no time left, we can't even pray.
There is nothing left to save us, for we are already in our graves.
The Devil has spoken, he had said to stop all of the pain.

The end it's coming, maybe we should try to stop it.
Our deaths have come, and we didn't even know it.
Our lives were already over, before the story even begun.
The truth it is coming, right after all of our pointless wars are won.

On the Streets

Stumbling still upon these long streets.
To where I am heading, I just don't know.
Maybe I'm searching for forgiveness.
Maybe I'm trying to just let the memories go.

I'm on the streets again, I've been walking for so many miles.
My feet they are bleeding, burning as if they were on fire.
But maybe in the end, I truly did deserve all of this.
Falling down on the road again, *melting into the tar.*

Stumbling still upon these endless streets.
To where I've been heading, I just don't know today.
Maybe I'm just trying to accept all of the blame.
Or maybe I've been trying, to escape from my shame.

My Dick In Her Mouth

Against the brick and our dreams they fall.
We cut in deep and don't care at all.
We are the sinners, we are the indulgent beasts.
Against the brick goes our madness, and we laugh all the same.

She was a demon, which wanted to eat my soul.
She wanted me to be hers, and to never let go.
I was a monster, in which only wanted pleasure.
I am just laughing, here with my dick in her mouth.

Against any logic, we leap and fall down the rabbit hole.
We land then upon a mushroom, and now it's eating our very souls!
We are the sinners, "*I am the monster, in which you hate.*"
It is all for pleasure, "my dick in her mouth" *and she loves how it tastes...*

Can You Now?

Can you please pull the trigger?
Come on my love just kill me now.
Can you please just end my life?
Cause all I want is to just get out.
So take me out now and end my pain.
End all of this torment of my past mistakes.
Please just kill me so I can no longer exist.
Take all of the pain away and what of me is left?
Can you now just pull the trigger and walk away.
Come and end me my love and then wipe away your tears.
Can you please just take my life and throw it away.
Can you now kiss my lips, so I can awake?

Yes It's Gonna Bleed...

Cut right in and tear inside.
I guess it's true that we're all blind.
We can't escape this endless war.
So we hide right there behind an open door.
It is so pointless, but still we have the nerve to try.
As looking into our past, cutting open my eyes.
Yes it's gonna bleed, out all in which I have seen.
And if you cannot take it, best leave it up to me.
I guess it is true that we will never escape this hell.
Maybe there is hope though, but we don't know where.
So I guess we are fucked, and that *Truth* will never change.
My heart is cut open, and yes it's gonna bleed...

As We Drown Together

Try your best to keep your head above the waves.
Hold your breath cause it won't take long before we fade.
As we drown together, I begin to wonder.
What if we had not let go, and had stayed ashore.
Would we have still drowned, alone in ourselves?
As we drown together, I have only to say.
I truly am grateful, that you are here at my side.

Distorted Recollections

Blood it has inked, this tome of our distorted past.
Maggots rain from the sky, and God he just laughs.
I think I am dreaming, awake here for so many ages.
I think this is Armageddon, smile as we are ending our world.

From the sky falls destruction, burning acid rain.
Like a dead man remembering, the deal with the Devil he had made.
I think that I'm a sleeper, whom dreams of only to wake.
I am a poem, etched into your flesh with a rusted blade.

Decay of my memories, but still I try to hold on.
Sanity has forsaken me, so I laugh as I nod back and forth.
Our world it has ended now, and we move on all the same.
All my memories of life are distorted *but I'll cherish them beyond the grave.*

Friendships & Failures

Can you remember, what we had said at the end of the hall?
Death had then come to take our souls.
The hour had passed, and we became but a dream.
And to this day I still wish to hold on, and not admit that we had failed.

Can you remember, when I had fought to save the day?
Can you remember, when I told you that I would never leave again?
I wish I could let go, and gaze up at all the beautiful stars.
But I am beyond darkness now, lost in a void with no light.

Such shame upon the conclusions, to all of my *friendships & failures.*
Can you remember, *when I had said that I'll love you until the end of time.*
I wish that I could remember, something other than despair.
And to this day I still wish, to not admit that we had failed.

"Sorry my friend..."

The Moon Gives To Me

The moon gives to me, hope that tomorrow might be saved.
This war has given me, nothing more than eternal pain.
My pride has given me, the option to stand and rise.
My death has given me, a chance to look the Devil in the eyes.

And I sincerely mean it, when I say that we are dead.
In life we were happy, but then it all just fades.
The moon she gives to me, hope for another day.
My death has given to me, the chance to slap God in his face.

Then I tell him to erase me, for I do not deserve this pain.
Again God speaks to me, and tells me that I'll be okay.
Still the moon she gives to me, a love I have never known.
As death takes me away, still the moon keeps my soul.

What Have They?

Demented reasons dancing about within a hollow mind.
Wretched voices speaking deep in me.
And what have they to say?
That we are falling now.
Into a reality of pain.

Demented creatures crawling around below my flesh.
They altogether connect themselves to me.
And what have they to say?
That we are awake now.
In a reality so insane.

Demented now and always until the very end of time.
For hours we all scream into the night.
And what have we to say?
That we are all thrown away...
Into a reality that exists no more.

Remember The BloodStain...

It was a harsh point you tried to make.
Alone in the back room, screaming in anger and rage.
For I am a bastard, the son of a bitch that you hate.
And after all of these years, still I remember the bloodstain.

Maybe it was a lesson that had to be learned.
And she was waiting there alone in that back room.
Screaming at the top of her lungs, in hurt and in rage.
Yes I do wish I could forget it, that Goddamned bloodstain.

It was a harsh point she had tried to make.
Alone in the back room, and there her soul still remains.
And yes I am the monster, in which I encourage you to hate.
Still to this day I wish to forget it, the blank look upon her dead face.

We Are The Lost

Tongue-less screaming, to the other side of then.
Razors rain from the sky, and seeping into our flesh.
We are ending our world, and we all just laugh.
We are the lost, truly we are all that is left.

We need to be strong, so that we can tear down the walls.
Let justice stand true, and catch us when we fall.
Our world is dead now, and there is nothing we can do.
We are the lost, and the only truth that remains.

Heartless weeping, frozen tears into her grave.
Razors rain from the sky, altogether they then flood my mind.
And no matter what, I cannot ease the pain.
Of the truth that we are the lost, and forever shall remain.

Cannibalistic

Tearing down into the bones.
Screaming now, "I'm all alone!"
It is over now, and thrown away.
We are starving now, fueled on only rage.

There is no stopping, our ever-growing hatred.
There is nothing to satisfy, what it is we crave.
Only murder can calm, all of the voices in my brain.
I am starving to death, but I won't let it end this way.

Digging down, straight to the bones.
Screaming so loud, "I am all alone!"
It is over now, and I live on to say.
That I will survive, "*no matter what it takes...*"

The Dead Are Rising

The sky is dead now and our futures are lost.
Our world has ended and no one seemed to care at all.
The time it is coming and we'll soon reach an ends.
The dead are rising and *of our flesh they will eat.*

Our hearts are forever frozen, alone weeping in pain.
Our minds they are dying, so nothing left to say.
Our world it has ended and we all just laughed.
The dead have all risen, and they will eat of our flesh.

We are all screaming and hoping that we might be saved.
The sky it is dead now and left eternally stained.
The time has come I say and we will always remember what they said.
The dead they have risen, and we will control this world again...

Beautiful Endings

Looking back upon all of the beautiful endings of my past.
I start to wonder, when my story will truly begin.
And I can't seem to fight away the tears...
I still can't seem to hide away all of my shames and fears.
But I do know now, that a kiss can mean more if only you just let it.
I do know now, that saying goodbye will always break my heart...
Looking back now upon all of the beautiful ending of my past.
And after all of the pain and bloodshed, I have now to only laugh.
Because the truth is that I did care, and I wanted us to be happy.
But then I learned, that you were always happier when I wasn't there.
So I do know now, that a kiss can mean more if both truly mean it.
I do know now, that saying goodbye was the right choice to make...

The Highway Calls

It's getting late and I think that I need to start heading home.
It's kind of cold, but I'm sure that I'll make it there in time.
It's starting to rain, so I just laugh and take a cigarette out of my coat.
I light it up and then start walking, across town towards my home.

The highway is calling, it wants me to stand upon it for another time.
The highway is yearning, to know what it is that drives me this time.
Into the nowhere that is my so very troubled heart and mind.
What has become of me, I am but only *a forgotten riddle behind the rhyme.*

The highway is calling, it wants me to hurry and get home.
It is so cold out this morning, and still so many miles to go.
My heart it is dead now, so I don't really feel as cold.
So what have I to say now, upon this highway as I walk?

It's getting late and I think I need to start heading home.
It's kind of dark out, raining and so very cold.
But I have to get out, and leave this place in my past.
The highway is calling, and ready to lead the way...

Further Than Death Now

All was set and ready for another epic chapter.
Now I've come to a point, where I no longer have control.
I do believe that I am failing you, but soon enough all shall know.
That I am so far out, further than death now and any thoughts of a soul.

These words will be spoken, and held true to our lost dire hopes of peace.
All that can be said I know I have saved, poetic truths hidden in each page.
Such a wretched notion, groping from within my tattered heart.
Soon shall all speak of me, as nothing more than a poet's ghost.

I am back now at our endings, still waiting for this all to begin.
I can only hope that someday you'll remember, what it is in which I said.
Do hold on as long as you can, until only the bliss of release is suffered.
We are all further than death now, still waiting for our lives to begin.

Cutting Out (*Shards of The Past.*)

I cannot sleep through this brilliant tormenting sickness.
I cannot weep, for all emotions in my heart have died.
I want to scream, I want to cry, I need to leave, this place behind.
As I cannot control, all of the twisted voices that dance inside my brain.
I lie here cutting out shards of the past, hoping to ease some of the pain.
But never does any form of peace reach my cold and broken heart.
And again I scream frozen in pain, constantly reopening old scars.
I just wanted her to know, *that there might have been a chance for hope.*
But sadly "*my love*" it was all just a dream and we need to awake...
Maybe somewhere beyond all the stars in our beautiful night skies.
Into a perfect hallucination of what lies hidden, upon the other side.
So now we have only this infinite torment, *Oh such blissful perpetual pains.*
And here I lie cutting out shards of the past, just trying to erase my face.
I never did exist in her world, *I was but a dream lost upon the sands of time.*
I never did exist in this world, *I was but a fragment of a broken whim.*
So again all is a miss, left hidden under the open stitch.
As here I am still cutting out shards of the past.
Just hoping that someday, I might get a chance to rest...

Again With This..?

Again we fall, into the unknown.
A million miles below all of the ashes and snow.
Into a place where not even our God can reach.
Again we fall, beyond this life and into another twisted dream.

Again with this! "All of the cutting into the flesh."
Again with this! "The tearing inside to find nothing is left."
Again with this! "All of the echoing laughter as we fall."
Again with this torment! "Left to be forever within our souls..."

She Betrayed Me For...

Ready now to take that moment and let it die.
Ready now to awake from the nightmare and rip out my eyes.
For she was the greatest thing that had ever happened in my life.
She was the death of my heart in which I shall cherish for all times.

We were the ones that were left hidden behind the curtains.
We were the last to ever see the world before it came to an end.
We had looked each other in the eyes, but nothing was said.
She had betrayed me for no better reason than, "*she wanted me dead...*"

Life Of Bliss

Wandering endless miles upon this road of leaves.
And into tomorrow is hidden the truth of what they say.
Smile my love as we are laughing, in this life of bliss and pain.
So take my hand now and let us all just fade away...

Far out and weeping, with only hatred left in this tired soul.
And as she kissed my lips, I felt a chill straight to the bones.
Then I open my eyes to see, that still I'm alone.
Left out here weeping, just wishing that I had the strength to let go...

Wandering for endless miles upon this beautiful road of leaves.
Just try to open your eyes, *so you can see the truth which shall always be.*
Locked forever and thusly left hidden, beneath a frozen lake.
Within this life of bliss, hatred, anger, death and pain...

Mixed Up & Fucked!

It's up to us to end this strive.
Still to this day I hold your rusted knife.
Within my chest, inside my dead heart.
So leave me be, for I wish to remain torn apart.

So shove that nail in and scramble my brain.
Mix it up and I'm fucked all the same.
Then try your best, to just look away.
I'm so mixed up, and fucked I shall forever stay.

So it's up to us to end all of our pains and strives.
Still to this day, the LSD it floods my spine.
As within my dreams, hides all the answers we seek.
So I guess we're fucked, and that is how it shall always be.

So beat me down and tie me up.
Slit my wrist and pour it into a cup.
Just add some lime and a bit of ice.
You drink it up, because it tastes real nice.

I'm so mixed! Beaten, broken and not to be fixed.
I'm so fucked! Thrown away and shit out of luck.
I am drained now, and you did love how sweet tastes.
But I am a poison, all mixed up, *"So I guess you fucked yourself today..."*

Ready To Drink the Poison

I am ready to take that final step over the edge.
I am ready now to admit that we have failed and our world is dead.
We are screaming and dreaming of finding peace.
We are all dead now, still waiting to release.
So all is enraged and soon to be calm...
"History is again repeating itself."
So come now and let us sing along.
I am ready to take God's hand and follow him beyond the flames.
I am ready to let it all go, "I just want to be saved."
We are all ready to drink the poison now.
As upon God's laughter we all fade away...
"Far beyond peace."

80

Her Eyes Were Golden

Her eyes were golden, right as the sun would begin to set.
Her voice it still haunts me, even far beyond death.
Her touch was so soothing, as she held me so close.
Her words meant the world to me, yet now we are but ghosts.

Just trying to remember something more than rage.
Trying to forget each other, lost behind a hidden page.
It was true love I say, but it all is lost deep in the past.
Still I try to hold on, to a forgotten memory which is dead.

Her thoughts were beautiful and were ever so pure.
Her voice it still haunts me and I wish it to remain, forever more.
Her kiss was my everything, more precious than my next breath.
Her eyes were golden, right as the sun would begin to set...

"Spark It Up!"

Here we go, let's end this test.
Blood it flows from this chest.
From the open wound where my heart should be.
I am the lost and forgotten sense of the thought.
Spark it up and let us reach to the other side of then.

Here we go again, let's end this fucked up world.
And as we are all burning together in the flames.
Tell me then what would we have to say?
Just let us go because I know we can find our own way.
Just as soon as we open our eyes to see our world was taken away.

Here we fucking go again, let's end this Goddamn test of sins.
As the blood is flowing, all hope is fleeting.
Here we go again, left alone on the ground, just weeping.
And we are to soon justify, all of the endless points of rage and sin.
Spark it up to end the pain, so here we go, again and again...

Fucked Away

All I have ever loved has been fucked away.
As I stare into the mirror, I know that I'm insane.
Screaming into the endless void!
"Get me out, get me out!"

All I truly am at this moment is nothing but fucked away.
All I have ever loved is dead now and no one cares.
So I go on screaming and screaming.
Let me out of the Goddamn cage!

All I have ever loved has been fucked away.
As I look so deep into your eyes, it reflects me so insane.
So I go on endlessly screaming into the void.
"Get me out, get me out, of this hell in which I made!"

Millions of Voices

Millions of voices screaming inside my brain.
Eating me from the inside out, so I guess it's all the same.
The hours are passing and nothing is left but shame.
We are all forsaken, left to die alone and in pain.

Our world it was beautiful, once upon a time.
Our minds were once pure, but now over the line.
Millions of voices are all screaming, echoing inside my brain.
Please get me out of myself, God just take me away!

To maybe a better chance of gaining, something much more.
And on we go tripping, through the unknown forever more.
With millions of voices speaking so enraged in my brain.
Please somebody just pull the fucking trigger!
"So I can get some sleep..."

Chapter 5

Silence Upon a Battlefield

Our Forgotten Love

Over passion it bleeds, left somewhere in the past.
This mind is running out of time, only a few more grains of sand.
As each chapter is filled, my heart becomes even more hollow.
Soon nothing of me shall remain, as never I did exist.

Her lips tasted like poison, forever taking hold of this mind.
I am just nothing, but a waste of poetic screams and cries.
Our forgotten love is dead now, someone took her away.
My love I can't hold on, so you weep as I begin to fade.

Over passion it was spoken, the truth of the death which lies in the past.
In time all shall understand, why it is that I can't keep looking back.
As each chapter is filled, my heart breaks and begins to die.
Soon nothing of me shall remain, *but only the truths hidden behind the lies.*

Speaking To the Ashes

Reach out to me my love, please take my hand.
"I am alone broken-bleeding on the floor."
Just a fragment, of a thought no longer remembered.
Take my hand my love, "*Then it all comes back to me...*"

I was a sad child, bleeding alone out in the rain.
Darkness filled my heart, and still to this day.
It hurt so dear, to watch as my love was burnt away.
Still to this day I speak to the ashes, "*And they tell I'll be okay...*"

Come back to me someday, and take me out of this hell.
Please just let me forget, all of the pains in which I've felt.
The loss of love and happiness too, "*So please my love, take me with you...*"
I just want this damned war to soon be over.

I was lost out in the rain, wandering for ages.
I was lost out there, just pleading for God to take us.
So very far away from all of the darkness of my dead heart.
Still I speak to the ashes, "*And they tell me that it will all be okay...*"

Awake In Death

Awake in death and forgotten in life.
Drugs filling my lungs, hate flooding my mind.
Demons waiting for a chance to take my soul.
Forever they will wait, to take their hold.
And God is laughing, because we need to but open our eyes.
Awake in our deaths, sleeping through our whole lives.
As hoping for an ending, only to find more questions.
What has become of me, "I just don't know"
Maybe it's a twisted sanity, left frozen to the bone.
And it's just a better chance for tragedy.
As we both wait to awake from this damn dream.
Lost in the darkness of our own lives.
Awake in death, and forgotten over time...

Hair-Trigger

These eyes are bleeding, these thoughts are screaming.
Our lives are fleeting, all hope is leaving.
There is now only hate, only pain.
Still I wish, that I could just walk away.

So I place the barrel against my forehead and smile.
As all my hopes were left behind, so many miles.
Still to this day we cannot deny it, all of the anger and pain.
So I place my finger on the trigger, ready now to seize the day.

And my heart is growing cold, this thought is getting old.
I just want to escape, this dark and tormented place.
To maybe find what it is that hides on the other side of the light.
So I squeeze the trigger, and just hope that all will be fine.

These eyes are bleeding, my heart still screaming.
Soon it will be over and silent through the night.
My thoughts are breaking, my heart is racing.
As I pull the trigger, and all goes silent...

When the Blood Falls

The blood it is gushing from the open wound in the wrist.
Echoing laughter reminding us, of that very last kiss.
Pushing far beyond that notion, and what have I to say?
As the blood is falling and filling this hollow grave.

It was taken back then to a better chance of knowing.
We are torn into pieces, now the blood is overflowing.
Yet we only wanted, this nightmare to make sense in the end.
But now it does, and we can never be the same again.

So please somebody wake me, and let us go.
Please my love just hate me, for leaving you buried under the snow.
"I never wanted to let you go," but that is how this story unfolds.
So what have we now, other that an open gash.

The blood it is gushing and it won't stop bleeding.
The pain it is gone now, so I might just have been dreaming.
Of a time when we were the weak, lead upon such bad intentions.
When the blood falls from off the razor, *maybe then we'll find some hope.*

We Take the Blade

War continues still to this day.
War has never ended.
No matter what they say.
Death has taken over.
Then we all together died.
We've all come so far out to see.
So please just open your eyes.

We take the blade and then cut off our face.
To prove the point that pain is all the same.
We have reached out to find that we have all failed.
And no matter what we do still we will burn in hell.

War continues still to this day.
And on the world moves with a smile on its face.
Oblivious to the general facts of our dismay.
So I guess we have only now.
To take up the blade...

87

Atomic Satan

The notion rises and breaks down all that ever mattered.
Her words still haunt us, hidden behind all the chatter.
The end is coming, and we just cannot wait.
We are all but dust and ash now, forgotten upon the dismay.

Our world has ended and no one seems to care.
Is it hopeless to think, that God is still out there.
The time has come and we have only to step into the graveyard.
And admit to the fact and we are all truly dead.

The atomic Satan, he has spread destruction across the lands.
Our toxic heartaches, taking their hold once again.
In pain it's all remembered, the fact of the lies in which we lived.
Now any chance for hope is over, and we burn away with all our sins.

The notion raises and breaks down all that has ever truly mattered.
Our bones begin to break, and it begins to sound like thunder.
The end has passed us now, and we all did fear the atomic Satan.
We are all but dust and ash now, just ghosts trying not to remember.

Child Of Rage

There it goes, steaming and boiling over the edge.
Please my friend try to kill me, bring the pain to an end.
I don't know what it is that I have done to deserve any of this.
Please somebody try to wake me, before it's too late.

I just want to be alright again, as I was once in the past.
I just want to get away from here, and to never again look back.
Please my friend just kill now, "this pointless child of rage."
And here we go again, stumbling onto another page.

There it goes, screaming as it begins to step over the ledge.
Please my friend just kill me, "I'm not gonna ask you again!"
I need to just stop this, Goddamn eternal pain.
So here I go again, moving on, as the child of rage...

Twisting Colors

Have not the mind to place it.
Have not the time to waste it.
Have not a chance to see.
Have no more air to breathe.

There is only death.
There is no more light.
All the colors are twisting.
But it's all in my mind.

Have not the mind to place it.
Have no more time to waste it.
Have not the strength to change it.
Have now only pain and grief.

There is only hate now.
There is only rage now.
All hope has died in my heart.
The beautiful colors are twisting, but it's all in my head...

Toxic Kisses

No chance left, only toxic kisses.
No hope left, only death and pain.
No one's left, I am alone out here today.
No one's left now, so we got what we wanted.

Fuck all of this torment that has been plaguing this mind.
Fuck all of you, I just want this world to die.
Please just let me fall now, so the rest of you can move on.
What of me is left now, I just don't seem to know.

For there is no chance left, only death and toxic kisses.
She wanted me to die, so she got what she was wishing.
No one's left now, I am all alone out here today.
No one's here with me now, but that's how we wanted it to be.

Eyes Forsaken

When I look into her eyes I see the Devil in my face.
Demons hounding me, because they want my soul.
I'm left here forsaken, "*Staring into her eyes!*"
And it won't get out, all the thoughts of her demise.

It's time we just let go and try to breathe.
It's time now for us to step onward and open our minds to see.
That death has taken over, "as the Devil puts his hands on me."
It is only the memory of her smile, which gets me through the pain.

"*Oh God! Here it goes again...*"
Hearing the voices in my head, helping me to tell, "I'm burning in hell!"
Still wishing that she could see, what has now become of me.
But I know I must just let go of the pain, and try to see.

When I look into her eyes I see the true death of my faith.
Demons shouting from deep within my soul.
We are all forsaken, "*And still I'm staring into her eyes.*"
Trying to forget the truth of our demise.

"*Oh God those Eyes...*"

If I Could Go Back

If I could go back, "What would I try to fix?"
If I knew then what I know now, could I make any difference?
Maybe I would try my best, to save our dead love.
Or maybe I would do just exactly what I've already done.

Just to say that I have lived it all once again.
If I could go back, would I stop myself from walking away?
If I could go back, could I correct all of my mistakes?
Like the time when I said that I wouldn't love you beyond that day.

If I could go back, "What would I try to fix."
If I could go back, *would I simply just be happy to once again see her face?*
If I could go back, I know that I would do my very best.
To tell her as much as I could - "*that, I'll always love you...*"

Fanatically Moving On

Like it's programmed into my brain.
Again I find myself, fanatically moving on into fate.
Yet I just smile as I let go and begin to fall.
Then I question, "*Why did I even, care at all.*"

I just need to move on, and out of this damned war.
I need to escape this place, and feel only bliss forever more.
I want to be happy, in the knowing that I will no longer exist.
I just need to move on, and leave all my pains in the past.

Somehow, it's almost like it was programmed into my brain.
The grim knowing of the fact that I will die alone someday.
Then I can be forever at peace, out there all alone.
So I just smile now, as I begin to let it all go.

It's almost like it was meant to end up this way.
It's almost like I enjoy all of the agonizing pains.
Again I find myself, fanatically moving onward into fate.
And it only raises more questions like, "*Why did I even, care at all?*"

Excruciating Memories

I cannot forever hide it.
I will never fully deny it.
The truth of a love that is dead and buried.
God I just want all of these memories to leave me be.

I still remember, when she told me to just hold on.
I can remember, when she smiled at the worst of times.
I can still remember, when I held her so tight in my arms.
I know now only pain, as I lie here bleeding alone.

I cannot forever hide it.
I never did deny it.
The fact that I was the one who killed my love.
So I take all of these memories, and load them into my gun.

"God please save me..."

She Loved Me Once

She loved me once but I just pushed her away.
She wanted me to be happy, but still she wanted me to stay.
I needed to get out, because hell was fast approaching our way.
She did once love me, "*God, why did I just push her away..?*"

It was a time of constant battling everyday.
It was a hellish purgatory in which I had made.
There was no hope, of ever saving any chance.
But she loved me once, but now alone I stand.

She was a fighter, so strong willed and ready to go.
She was my greatest reason, as to why I'm still here.
I needed to just get out, before I destroyed all I ever loved.
But that war is over now, and neither of us won...

"*Forgive me...*"

Losing the Sands Of Time

Nothing's left now, only ashes and dismay.
Where have we been all these years?
Lost so deep and out in the abyss of space.
Counting each grain of sand from within the hourglass of time.

Nothing's left to save us, we have all been deserted.
Please mother, "Wake me now!" Because I know I don't deserve this.
To be lost out here in space, where not even God can reach.
Losing the sands of time, so what now is left of me?

We've been forgotten, so we are on our own.
The end is coming, and now it's getting cold.
As I am to be forever left alone out here lost deep in space.
Losing the sands of time, and they are never to be replaced...

Passion Fading

All at once, everything I ever loved just faded away.
Into the unknown, that is where I hide in my dreams.
God I want to just end this and awake from my own tormented hell.
All of my passions faded away, as my world came undone.

Is there any chance left, for us to say, we'll love each other to the end of time.
My love I wish you were here right now, to see what I've become.
Just a forgotten man remembering a time when our lives were surreal.
Now all the passion I held in my heart is dead, and buried under the hill.

We need to just leave now, "there is no saving today."
All at once, everything I had ever loved just faded away.
So please erase me, burn me until I am but dust and ash.
For all my passions are dead now, "but I'll love you always in our past..."

For Demons I Speak

Can you hear me whispering from inside your brain?
I am the voice that reminds you that you truly are insane.
I speak for demons, angels, Gods and the Devil himself.
I am the voice, here to remind you, that you're going to hell.

Can you hear the death of hope out there, in our dying world?
Can you hear all the screaming, as our world begins to burn?
I am here to tell you, that all along you've been insane.
I am here to tell you, that I'm never going to go away.

I speak for demons, angels, Gods and the Devil himself.
I am that part of you, that you wish would remain, locked in hell.
I am the biggest part of you, that you wish would just die.
I speak for the demons when I say, *"everything will be just fine."*

Our Misplaced Hearts

Yes my love I'm still torn apart, searching for our misplaced hearts.
In time we might understand, something more than this pain.
Please my love, kill me now, and let me then just fade away.
There we might find our misplaced heart, left in hell where they should stay.

I feel so unguided, no direction to this torment.
I just want to let it all go, and then enjoy the fall.
But no matter what I say at all, you will hate me just the same.
My love how could you have done this, just thrown our hearts away.

Yes my love I'm still torn apart, left out here with only our broken hearts.
In time we might understand, why it is that we did fail.
And our hearts were then forever, banished to hell.
Where here my love, I shall forever hold our hearts...

The Sky Fills With Death

Extensively anticipated damned lives left burning.
Watch as the angels weep as the sky fills with death.
Listen to the voice as it speaks to you and tells you nothing is left.
Only hatred, only anger, only pain, only rage...

Come with me and let us leave this damned metaphoric cage.
And journey to a place far beyond our dying world.
A place where smiles and laughter still remain.
Let us leave behind the pains of a pointless war...

The sky fills with death and we are all to blame.
Our mother Earth is dying, and we laugh all the same.
Try to listen to the voice, which is telling you that nothing is left.
Only hatred, only anger, only pain, as our sky it fills with death...

"Please open your eyes, so that you can see..."

I Am That Evidence

Bring to me a more dire thought of our end.
Take me back to purgatory, so I can resolve all my sins.
Cut deep into me and watch then as all the blood spills.
It is black now, for all this time I must have been dead.

Bring to me a more true sense to the facts in which we fear.
Hold onto me as long as you can, "I think I'm gonna die..."
Please let me be something more than only a failure that tried.
Let me tell you how much I love you, but you won't open your eyes.

I am that evidence in which was left behind at the scene of the crime.
You were the only one that was there, to laugh as I died.
I just want to go home now, and leave all of this torment behind.
I am that evidence in which to this day you still hide...

Bring to me a more dire thought of our tragic ends.
Let me tell you how much I loved you, before I was thrown away again.
And in this purgatory I still wish there was a way I could say *"I tried!"*
But I shall always remain as the evidence in which you still hide...

Standing Up (*For the Weak.*)

Once again I will take that hit against my cheek.
I'll be right here, standing up for the weak.
Ready to fight for those who need strength.
I'll always be right here, ready and willing to save the day.

Here I stand now, taking that hit against my face.
And I watch as the blood drips off my flesh and into the dirt.
I'll always be right here, ready to be strong for the weak.
I will be the one, to stand tall and save the day.

Once again I'll take that brutal hit against my face.
I'll be right here, standing up for the weak.
Ready and willing to fight until the bitter end.
I'll always be right here for you, ready to reach out and save the day...

A Pencil In My Hand

Where does all the pain go? So gentle you press the blade.
Where did all my faith get me? Six feet under and in my grave.
Where did God go? Maybe he had enough of this sick joke.
Where did my world go? Lost somewhere in all the smoke.

And it is then pressed below the flesh.
Digging deep into the palm of my hand.
I feel now only pain and regret.
Because I know that fate has now come for me.

This is such a twisted dream. Infesting my troubled mind.
There is no chance of saving me. So please don't waste your time.
Truth and agony still ringing. Pressing far beyond the pain.
A pencil in the palm of my hand. *Injecting poetic-nonsense into my brain.*

"On I bleed, and no one cares..."

Puking Up Rust & Ash

"It is noon..." I think I'm dying.
"It is cold..." So very silent.
"It is dark..." But I know it's all in my head.
"It is time now..." So life was but a vivid dream.

Violently tearing, fingernails digging into my face.
This world is over, and starting now once again.
The demon is laughing, because this is what he wasn't.
I think I'm dying, so I laugh as I watch myself coming undone.

"It is noon..." I think I'm frying.
"It is cold..." Forever so very silent.
"It is dark here..." But I know this is all just in my head.
"It is time now I believe..." So all along I guess I've been dead.

So please just kill me.
Take me away from here.
Please just fucking kill me!
Stop me from all this puking up the rust and ashes of her grave...

The Clove Remembers

My eyes are burning, my head is hurting, this room is spinning.
"Fuck I need to find some sort of a better grip."
Damn I think I am truly sick, as I lie here weeping on the floor.
Only cold-darkness to hold me, uncouth through the night.

The clove remembers, that beautiful painting on the wall.
The picture of grace and beauty, a place of true love and peace.
The clove can remember, a time when we were both young and free.
A time when we embraced only the dream of loving each other Always & Forever.

My body is shaking, my head is still aching, this room is spinning...
"Fuck! I need to find some sort of a better grip."
It truly hurts, as I watch this blue rose bloom just beneath the wrist.
No, I cannot deny that I am ready now to just fade away.

For she shall never forgive me, not for what I've done.
Still the clove can remember, a time when the two of us were one.
A time when we were happy, to just be at each others side.
But now I can feel only this bitter cold, so uncouth through the night...

Untruth She Whispered

My muse did whisper her toxic notions into me.
And to this day I just can't let go of the pain.
She was all that I had ever loved in my life.
She was the only reason I had left, as to why I still breathe.

Untruth she whispered, and it remains still in my dead heart.
My muse was so great to my eyes, but now I'm blind and torn apart.
She was all that I had at that time, but still she smiled and left.
As I stood there waiting alone in the cold.

My muse did whisper, all of her toxic notions into me.
As to this day, I just want to set my broken heart free.
She was everything to me, once upon a memory lost.
Untruth she whispered, and it remains forever in my dead heart.

This Face Doesn't Exist

This face doesn't exist, it was only a dream.
Please wake up now my love, so I can set you free.
I am nothing but a dead man in truth, just burnt ash.
I never did exist at all, I was nothing but a sad dream.

This heart does not exist anymore, it is rotten and full of tar.
My mind can't fix it this time, so now it's another deep scar.
Please God find and save me from all of this pain.
This face doesn't exist my love, because it was taken away.

It is my fault that our world feels both fear and pain.
It is my fault that our love came to an end on that day.
Please forgive me, for not saying sorry sooner my love.
This face doesn't exist, because I was only a small part of her sad dream.

My Soul Torn to Shreds

My heart still remembers what it is that God had said.
That my past and future are both to remain forever dead.
So the angels all laugh, as my soul is torn to shreds.
There is just nothing I can do, to stop you from weeping.

And my memories are dying upon all of my un-waking dreams.
My heart is broken, as I lie here listening to the voices in my head.
I love this feeling of bliss, as I am here bleeding out all of me.
My soul torn to shreds, so there is nothing that remains to see.

My words echo on still, deep in the abyss of my own forgotten hell.
Love-Notes to a dead-girl, reminding me of how I once felt.
My heart can no longer take this, I need to get the fuck out!
I feel only as if my soul is torn to shreds, *but I need to keep telling myself.*
"It's all - just in my head..."

That God Said...

Devil-whispers sneaking over the lips of a beautiful little angel.
She speaks of a truth that could bring an end of times.
What of mankind, in this conspiracy beyond divinity.
Our dead world still it remembers what it is that God said...

As gravity is shoving us down into the dirt.
Try to remember what it is that made us real.
Speak now of that dire truth my little angel.
And upon those words our world burns away.

Evil notions left echoing within the heart of a little beautiful angel.
She knows the truth of a conspiracy that could bring the end of times.
Satan just sits there and waits, "because he knows us just that well."
Our dead world it still remembers, what it is that God had said.

As faith is there tearing into the middle of the wrist.
Soon enough all of this pain will be but a miss.
As our whole world just burns below our very own feet.
Please God save us, from the agonies of defeat.
And we just fade away, as we remember what God said...

It Is Silent Now

It is silent upon the battle field.
Only ghosts wander this land.
I cannot let go of my pledge my love.
I shall someday be in your arms once again.

It is silent now upon this dead night.
Only ghosts remain of this tragic past.
No matter how far in this war we've come.
We are nowhere close to reaching an end.

It is silent upon the battle field.
Only time will tell, how we will reach the end.
It is silent now, here in this poets head.
But the war is far from ever being over.
In truth, *"I'm still waiting for it to begin..."*

Here I wait, silent in my mind.

Chapter 6

Beneath This Flesh

Insignificant Efforts

All my insignificant efforts go on to no avail.
With every day that passes I realize more that this is hell.
God can't save me, "I fucking did this to myself!"
Please somebody kill me, to end some of the pain...

All my efforts to protect this fragile world go on unheeded.
I am looked at as an insignificant waste of poetic pains and cries.
Please Satan listen to me, "Just get me the fuck out!"
And on moves this world, spinning onward without me...

All my insignificant efforts push on to no avail.
This place is getting colder, that's how I know it is hell.
But God can't reach me, because I'm not worth his time.
Please somebody kill me, so peace can be found within my mind.

"Please - somebody hear me..."

Miles From the End

Tell me my love, how many miles are we from reaching an end?
We've all come so far, through pains, joys, fears and sins.
And after all of this time, why is it that we still can't see the end to be?
Please my love, just hold me close and tell me that it will all be okay.

How far have we come down this road, tens of years and miles gone?
How long have these lyrics been in my head, and still I sing along?
I just want this war to come to an end, so we can all find release.
We have been fighting for decades now, and it was all done in the name of peace.

Still miles from the end, hoping that someday we will be set free.
How long have we been fighting this war, trying to improve our insanities?
And after all of this time, why is it that we still can't see an end to be?
Please my love, just hold me close and tell me it will all be okay...

"Still – miles to go."

"Our Dreams Are Dead Now."

Her eyes still haunt me, those memories won't fade.
Her lips have scarred mine, still I feel it to this day.
In my heart I am dead now, left somewhere in the past - betrayed.
In the truth of reality, our dreams are dead - *now and always*.

Oh fuck this torment that is feasting on my lost hopes.
So I guess I'll just admit it, that I was all along just a ghost...
I am a shadow that is left in the darkness of space and time.
I guess I was nothing more than a backwards truthful-lie.

Her words are still here, haunting my weak soul.
Her eyes still hold me, freezing me down to the bone.
In my heart I am dead now, just like all of our pointless dreams.
So fuck this endless nightmare, we know only as reality...

"Our dreams are dead..."

Birth of My Torment

Faces of dead children screaming for God to save them.
Demons feasting, having their way with all our sins.
We are unforgiven for all our endless mistakes.
In death births my torment, driving me insane.

Fuck any logic, here in these backwards visions of delight.
Kill my heart now my friend, save me from myself.
Take me to a place, where I can return back to hell.
For I shall never forget, the truth of the life I did take...

I fucking murdered her, "I know my soul can never be saved."
Please just fucking kill me, "so I can finally leave this place."
Watch as the death of my heart comes, "birthing my endless torment."
I shall never be forgiven, "not after what I have done..."

Decaying In My Veins

Again in torment and it's all the fucking same.
Again I'm on the floor, screaming alone and in pain.
Again with this suffering, here in my broken mind.
Life decaying all around me, so I know that it is time...

So let us scream now, "we shall soon see the light!"
Let us forget the past, as we turn off the lights.
Come and take me, to some place I've never been.
Life is dead now, and it won't ever come back again.

Decaying within my veins, the memories of our love.
I only wanted to save you, "What the fuck, have I done!?"
Again here in torment and it's all the fucking same.
Again we are the dying, memories left in our shallow graves.

I just wanted to save our love, from ending the way it did.
So I failed you my dear, all over and again and again and again.
My life is dead now, lost in the darkness of our pains.
All my memories of her, they are left here decaying within my veins.

I Shall Eat Your Flesh

The murder of joy, "I know that the best."
I love the sound of your screaming.
As I begin to eat your flesh.

I shall always cherish the taste of fresh blood.
I love the fear in your eyes as I sink my teeth in.
I shall eat your soul, your body and your heart of sins.

The death of sanity, "I can remember that the best."
I love the sound of your screaming.
As I make you watch me eat of your flesh...

Drugs Flooding Me

Watch as this shell of a man breaks into pieces.
Laugh as I step over the edge and wave goodbye.
Catch me by my wrist as I'm falling, my love.
Tell me that you never cared as you let me go in spite.

I was never a great person, only a sad waste of time.
My existence once had a great meaning, but was lost over time.
These drugs are flooding me, so I believe I can bleed smoke.
There is no chance of you saving me, so you just cast me away...

Watch as this shell of a man, bleeds out his poetic heart.
Only for no one to ever care, for this dead man's war.
Please find me in you, where I've been hidden all along.
Listen to the riddle, and don't get the lyrics wrong.

I was never much of a great person, only a tormented waste of time.
My existence once had a meaning, now lost behind the lines.
These drugs have taken over, my brain and tired soul.
My whole mind is flooded, now hell is growing cold.
"And it is I that holds all control..."

Anarchism

Resisting to all of your sick thoughts of control.
We are not sheep to be led straight to the slaughter.
We shall all together rise and bring your system down.
We shall watch it all burn, for then we shall be freed.

We will not take all of your sick views of pointless control.
We will not abide to these unfair laws of your system.
Let us burn the walls down, and smile over the flames.
Let us be truly free, in a way that no one can take it away.

Resisting to your entire one sided stance on government.
We will end these wars for once and for all.
We shall burn the world to the ground.
So there is nothing left for us to fight over.
"Then we shall truly be free..."

Divine Conflictions

God had whispered his heart into Satan.
Satan lost himself over the knowledge of the universe.
The angels all questioned and then fell from above.
Satan knew something was wrong, as reality came undone.

God wanted us to be happy, but we are still here at war.
God wanted us to love him, on and on forever more.
Satan wanted us all to listen, to the voice within ourselves.
Mankind cannot take this, we are too weak and overwhelmed.

Damn this divine conflict in which shall never end.
Damn the fires of hell, burning here beneath this flesh.
God please end all of this pain and torment within our minds.
Satan is dead now, because he ran out of time...

As I Told Her

As I told her, soon enough I will no longer exist.
As I told her, I will remember most our very first kiss.
As I told her, I will surely die alone.
As I told her, I sadly never did have a soul.

She once told me, that I was all she ever wanted.
She once told me, that we would be together *Forever & Always.*
She once told me, that I was all she needed at the time.
She once told me, to just let go and open my eyes.

As I told her, there is no chance of saving me.
As I told her, when we were together life was as a dream.
As I told her, my whole life is just an open book.
As I told her, I always knew that I would die alone.

"Pages blowing in the wind..."

Watching You Leave...

It hurt so much, watching you walk away.
It hurts still to this day, as endless goes all the pain.
Why can't you reach me, here in front of your eyes?
Just try to reach out to me, but now we're out of time.

As I was watching you leave, my heart began to break.
As now you are gone, I don't know what to say.
Is there any chance that we could just start over at some point?
I just need to realize, that my love for you is dead.

It hurt so much, as I watched you walk away.
I was only second best, just not good enough that day.
It hurts still to this day, to know how I've been treated.
And it hurts still, as remembering when you walked away.

Nativity

Remember fully the place in which I am from.
Remember the life I was born into.
Never forget my words and what all I have done.
Take me back to where this all began, the hell I am from.

It was a beautiful city, powerful and strong.
I was born into a great life, but it all came undone.
I am ready to go back now, to what I call home.
Take me back that my place of birth, where I won't be alone.

Remember fully the monster in which I am.
Remember the life I have taken, I am stained with that sin.
Never forget just who I am and where I'm from.
Let's go back to the beginning now, and end this for once.

Murder the Legitimacies

Time has taken the very best of me.
So I just weep as watching the murder of all legitimacies.
Can it make sense at some point, *"just for I..?"*
Lift then and see, behind the Devil's eyes.

Embrace not the movement of the needle.
Pleasure upon the agony of the blades in me.
What then will become of our dying reality?
Can maybe we ever stop these pointless rants?

Time has surely taken its hold of me.
So I just weep over the murder of all legitimacies.
We are left then with only hatred and miles to go.
Set-not and soon enough all will be on its way...

Embrace not the torment of the needles as they inject.
Now all matter in this mind, it is growing so sick.
We can't make it this time, we are going to fail.
We shall all weep over the death, of all in which we have ever felt.

They Have Fallen

They have fallen from the sky.
We are falling, and we don't know why.
They have reached the fingertips of God.
We are all banished, to the wastelands of Nod.

They have fallen from the stars.
We are digging, deep into these old scars.
They have felt the lips of the heaven's angels.
We are all damned, led upon pointless fables.

They have fallen down to the earth.
We are falling, and in hell we shall burn.
They have known all the answers this whole time.
We are the fallen, here waiting upon the other side...

Angels Of Immorality

The paint is dripping onto the blank canvas.
The picture is growing, an outline of my madness.
The angels are whispering, sweet motivations into my brain.
The picture is changing, with each breath I intake.

The smoke is lingering, remaining within my dead lungs.
To the core we are burning, now I feel so very numb.
Like in the past when I was *the zombie*, ready to take control.
The angels of immorality, still they hold my broken soul.

The paint is still flowing, filling the canvas with life.
My flesh is all gone now, cut off with their rusted knife.
In pain I am screaming, praying for all of this to just stop.
The angels are all laughing, painting the canvas with my blood.

The picture is overwhelming in its nature.
The paint is drying up, and soon all shall see.
That I am a piece of artwork, locked in forever and never to be free.
The angels are all weeping, because they know that they are me...

Set the Crown (*Upon the Leaves.*)

Ages of onward moving upon this road of leaves.
In times of war it is comprehended, the truths of our inevitabilities.
For as of now I truly am the king of this damned decaying world.
So take my crown and set it upon the fallen leaves.
Look me in the eyes and say, you always knew what was best for me.
Love me onward and until the eternal end of this rhyme.
Set the crown upon the leaves, and it is consumed over time.
Into the earth, where now I rest my mind today.
Hidden behind that open door, here beneath a frozen lake.
"Please love me my children, for I have died for your souls."
I am your king, the poetic monster that has taken control.
For ages and ages of pushing onward upon this road of leaves.
As on-top this hill I rest my head, just hoping for peace.
But these wars can never come to an end.
If we never learn to just set our hate free...

Mushrooms Beneath This Flesh

Take that razor and cut into my chest.
Rip my heart out and I scream out my last breath.
As our world is melting before my very eyes.
Smile with me Satan, let us enjoy our demise.

With anger steaming, lifeless dreaming of heaven's light.
In hatred screaming, as this body is burned alive.
It tastes like candy, the heroin that bleeds from my eyes.
The mushrooms are beneath my flesh, so I just might die...

For there is no saving a soul that did never truly exist.
Like fire it burns, the mushrooms growing beneath this flesh.
Oh let us sing this melody, all the way into our graves.
And upon another sunrise, we fritter away our faiths.

So take that razor and cut deep into my hollow chest.
Rip out my heart and I'll bleed out only tar and ash.
And I laugh as I watch our whole world decay before my very eyes.
Smile with me Satan, let us enjoy now our eternal demise...

A Dagger

Cutting deep into the middle of my aching eyes.
A dagger made of bone, from a golden demon's spine.
JUST SCREAM ALL THE WAY!
JUST BLEED OUT THE SHAME!
JUST CUT INTO ME!
JUST KILL ALL MY DREAMS!
As someday I shall receive the death I deserve.
And at some point or another I just hope that we learn...

"THERE IS NO SAVING ME..!"
"THERE IS NO SAVING ME..!"
"THERE IS NO SAVING ME..!"
"THERE IS NO SAVING ME..!"
"THERE IS NO SAVING ME..!"
"NO SAVING ME..!"
"NO SAVING ME..!"
"NO SAVING ME..!"

Lyrical Discords

So I do feel, that I've got to kill.
I've hurt myself, and gone to hell.
And just one more tear rolls down my face.
"God I'm a disgrace."

Fighting upon these lyrical discords.
Losing faith as I lie bleeding on the floor.
Just waiting for her to take my life.
Waiting for someone to turn off the lights.

And I do feel, that I've got to kill.
I'll hurt myself, and then go to hell.
And just one more tear rolls down my face.
"I'm just a fucking disgrace."

Screaming out here in the rain to our lord.
Lost upon these endless lyrical discords.
Here I am still, lying broken on the floor.
Just waiting for someone to turn off the light...

Fuck Your BullShit!

Poetic minds twisting into these side-set ends.
New views of darkness, growing upon tragic whims.
So fuck your bull shit! Your endless nonsense!
It's so confusing, all the hatred abusing.
This soul is burning, and still no learning.

Poetic lies twisting deeper into the said-not cries.
A new age of darkness, growing within my evil mind.
So fuck your bull shit! Pathetic nonsense!
It's so amusing, all of the tormented abusing.
Of this soul, in which has never learned...

In Flames I Wait

In flames I wait for God to tell me when.
In the past I was alone, as I am once again.
In pain I wait for the answer to the question unasked.
In some way or another I know that my life has passed...

In flames I wait for God to tell me why.
In my heart I know that I've been dead all my life.
In pain hides the notions, still so unseen.
In some way or another, I need to find release...

In flames I am burning, waiting for God to arrive.
In my own past I am forgotten, so I was but a lie.
In the darkness of a bitter idiocy, there is now only pain.
In some way or another, I've always been insane...

As on I burn here in these flames waiting for God to say.
In time I might be forgiven, but it will not be today.
In pain remains all of my efforts, dire and so very grim.
In flames I wait for the answers, to the questions unasked.

Affecting the Answers

Affecting the answers by changing the questions.
Changing the questions until no one can understand.
So open your eyes to see this world is no longer the same.
We once loved each other, but now in hell we stay.

Affecting the answers by changing the questions.
Changing the questions until only the Devil and God can understand.
Why is it that still to this day, we remain forsaken?
Soon enough we shall realize that we did never exist.

Affecting the answers by destroying the questions.
Destroying the questions and anyone who would understand.
So open your eyes now to see that our world we loved is dead.
We have changed the outcome, by creating a new question to ask.

Soft Lips

She pressed her soft lips against mine.
She whispered into my ear, telling me that I'll be fine.
She once loved me, upon a beautiful dream.
But we are awake now, in our own purgatories.

I kissed her soft lips to release myself from hell.
I told her that I'll always love her, so I guess I did fail.
She once told me, to just let go and fall away.
I did once love her, but now that emotion is thrown away.

She pressed her soft lips against mine.
I can still feel it, and I know it has been quite a long time.
She once told me, that I meant to her so very much.
So I kissed her soft lips, but then we both turned to dust...
"Now all I've loved has blown away."

Single-Handedly

On my own, I shall bring an end of times.
In my soul, remains more of a twisted rhyme.
Upon this anger, shall tomorrow show the way?
Inside of my skull is only ash where there should be a brain.

Single-handedly, I shall bring forth an end of time.
All together, the demons in my head spew up another rhyme.
Fueled on hatred, the rage that builds within my head.
And so very soon I know, that we will all be dead.

On my very own, I have the power to save our world.
In my hands I hold the answer, but I will never tell.
Of the truth in which we still fight for to this very day.
Single-handedly I shall dig myself, out of my own grave...

Wrecked & Laughing

Death has come and the pain is passing.
Where have we gone, we're wrecked & laughing.
Bleeding in horror, no chance of surviving this.
So we just laugh on and on, until our very last breath.

Death has spoken and he is ready to take our souls.
The Devil was watching, as we took that wrong turn.
Now pain is passing and coming to an end.
We are just bleeding now, away all that we were...

The end has come now and we just weren't ready.
Where are we going, somewhere that we'll be free?
We're bleeding out all of, what we were in our lives.
We're just wrecked & laughing, because now it is time.

Panicking!

Can't shake the fear...
GET ME THE FUCK OUT!!!
GET ME THE FUCK OUT!!!
I just know that I can't be right here...
PLEASE GET ME OUT!!!
GET ME OUT!!!

Can't stop this endless worry...
THE FEAR IS GROWING!!!
THE FEAR IS GROWING!!!
I know that it must just be all in my head...
PLEASE GET ME THE FUCK OUT!!!
GET ME OUT!!!
BEASUE I THINK THAT I AM DEAD!!!

"I'm dead..."

Just Leave Me

Just leave me here to rot and fade.
Leave me here in this open grave.
Forget me now and erase my face.
Forget me now and what have we to say?

Just leave me here in my own head.
Just leave me here because I am dead.
Just leave me be so that I can die.
Just forget me now and waste not your time.

Just fuck all memories of me that might remain.
Destroy whatever you find, here in my grave.
Never look back and just keep on moving.
Forget me now and please walk away.

Just leave me here to rot and fade.
Leave me uncovered, here in my open grave.
Forget me now and burn away my face.
Forget me now and what have we to say?

Mind-Set Breaking

Upon the dead leaves of a winter passed.
Within this heart it bleeds both tar and rusted ash.
We have come to take that motive and return it to God.
What a fucked up mind-set, but it's all I have left.

Upon eternal damnations felt all the way to the grave.
Spoken over the lips of the Devil, so grim we do say.
Driven further into these nightmares we cannot escape.
Fuck this damn mind-set, breaking me insane...

Upon the dead leaves of a winter passed.
We have awaited this moment and now it comes to pass.
Felt so brutal, digging into our now tattered souls.
So maybe that is why, God told us to just turn away...

Paying the Devil

Paying the Devil back, but only what I owe him.
I'm trying to get my life back, before it is over.
I need to get the fuck out! Of this sick twisted cage.
Here in my mind, an endless fucked up maze.

I'm paying the Devil back, for what I have borrowed.
It has been so long, sense I have taken his powers.
For I am truly evil, and the Devil just keeps count.
But I am paying him back for, all that I do owe.

God is pissed off, because I've seen the light of darkness.
Mankind does hate me, but that is nothing new.
I need to just get the fuck out! Of this sick demented cage.
It's time I got my life back, but the Devil expects to get paid...

Adored & Pristine

I can't fully describe her beautiful eyes.
I wish that I could just say that I love her.
So maybe I'll just give it some time.
Then at some point, this all might make some sense.

She told me that I was a great person.
But the world doesn't even consider me human.
She told me that I'm a fighter.
But the world beats me down because I am weak.

I can't fully describe her beautiful blue eyes.
I love her soothing voice, as it echoes within my mind.
So maybe someday I will prove, that I do in fact love her.
She truly is, all that my heart does desire...

Chapter 7

Partly Through

Substances Invading

Felt to the core, so very wasted.
Here on the floor, so very pasted.
Have not the energy to move anymore.
I feel I'm just so fucking wasted.

Substances invading, my head today.
My tongue is cut out, so what have I to say?
There is no getting out, I've done this to myself.
I can't feel my face, "I think that I've died."

Where am I today, this place I cannot describe?
Who am I in truth, just a dead man still waiting to die?
What have we left now, other than the drugs in our veins?
I feel so wasted, and fucked up I'll forever stay...

Felt to the core, beyond my tired soul.
Here I lie on the floor, weeping alone so cold.
I have not the motives, to reach out and change the script.
I feel like I'm about to die, "so I guess this is it..."

Insanity Identifies

No control, only endless amounts of laughter and rage.
No more of a soul, because you my love had taken it away.
No time left at all, so we set ourselves on fire.
No point to this madness, and it continues on all the same.

I was a child that only wanted, to be sheltered from evil.
I was lost out in the darkness, no way to escape from myself.
I was always just a little bit different, in the way that I am.
I am truly the definition, of insanity and control.

So is there anything left, there in that forgotten graveyard.
I had tried my best, but still I could not save us.
So maybe all along, all of this was just inside my own head.
I am truly a man of madness, ready to control our deaths...

Right Next to Me

Here I am, standing right next to me.
I am beside myself, and it feels so strange indeed.
As I cut in, and tear out all of what was inside.
Hold on my love, "I don't want you to die..."

And still to this day, I find myself standing right next to me.
It feels so strange, to watch myself cutting away at me.
To try and cure the sickness, found within my shattered heart.
I'll be right here the whole time, just tearing myself apart.

Here I go, leaning over the ledge and looking down.
I'm ready to let go, and leave all my pains out.
For they are growing, and soon to reach the surface.
Here I go again, losing track of who I truly am.

And still to this day, I find myself standing right here next to me.
Is there anything I can do, to ease up some of this insanity?
I begin to cut in deep, and start tearing out all that was inside.
Hold on my love, "I think you're gonna die..."

Sleep Deprived

I'm so very tired.
I've been wake for days now.
I feel so sick.
I'm think I'm gonna throw-up.
I need to end this war now.
I cannot rest until this is over.
I want to just sleep.
And dream all of my pains away.
I need to get some sleep soon.
Or I might go forever insane.
I'm so very tired.
I've been awake for so many days now.
I think I'm dying.
And nothing can change it.
I need to get some sleep now.
"Please now somebody wake me!!!"

Engraved Into My Skull

What is this symbol that's engraved into my skull?
Where are you taking me and why is it getting cold?
Is there any chance that I might one day awake?
What is this engraved into my skull, maybe it's my name.

So is there anything left now for us to hold onto?
This world is a desert, so very cold and damaged.
Please let me be more than just a nonsense, dancing upon our graves.
This thing that's engraved into my skull, tell me what does it say?

Lead us now upon that purpose, of seeing tomorrow's light.
Remember me forever, and all in life that I have said.
I do in fact truly love you, but you were all along just in my head.
So I smile, because I know now that we are nearing the end.

It's All Just Random

It's all just random, the things that are screaming in my head.
It's all been a fun trip, but now it must end.
We've come far in this journey, only to learn what we already know.
It's all so very random, the emotion I hide within my soul.

I need to get a tighter grip, before I slip away.
I need to kiss her lips, and tell her how I felt that day.
I need to stop fighting myself, because I'll never win that way.
I need to just stop this shit, and just fucking walk away.

It's all just random, the notions that go on within my head.
It's all been a great trip, but now we're reaching an end.
We've come far, but only to learn what we already know.
It's just so fucking random, the voices in my head, *"telling me I'm alone."*

A Storm Is Coming

It's getting dark out, and it just started raining.
It's getting cold out, and nothing can change it.
It's getting so dark now, I think a storm is coming.
We try to hold on, but now it is flooding.

We cannot stop this, all the changing of the times.
We cannot deny this, the pains within this mind.
It's so very dark now, the winds strong and growing.
It's raining harder, there is a storm a coming.

It's pointless to try and out run it, because we're out of time.
It's pointless to try and stop me, because I am only in your mind.
It's very dark now, the water is now flooding over our heads.
A storm is coming, and we'll soon enough all be dead.

No we cannot just stop this, all the hatred in our souls.
We cannot save us this time, now it's just too cold.
The winds are growing, and destroying everything in sight.
A storm is coming, but it's all just in our minds...

Faith Fleeting

Faith is fleeting, in hatred screaming.
As angels are weeping, dead upon our dreaming.
There is no stopping the bleeding.
We are all now burning in hell for all our sins.

As fate is creeping, in dreams it's sinking.
The Devil is weeping, here dead in my arms today.
For now what has God to say.
Only that we've come so far just to watch this story begin.

Faith is fleeting, in hatred still screaming.
As all the little angels are weeping, dead upon our dreaming.
There is no stopping the bleeding.
For we are now burning and we must pay for all our sins...

Insufferable

I can't take this shit, PLASE GET ME OUT!
I can't feel my face, I JUST WANT TO GET OUT!
This mind is gonna break, THEN WHAT THE HELL IS NEXT!?
I can't take this shit anymore, SO GET ME THE FUCK OUT!

Those words go on constant within this tired mind.
I've been doing this for so long now, it's just another rhyme.
I want to take my life back, and try to make a difference.
So I let you slit my wrist, so I can bleed out all the pain...

I can't take this shit, IT'S EATING ME TO DEATH!
I can't bare this strain, FELT HERE WITHIN MY CHEST!
My mind it is breaking, SO WHAT THE HELL IS NEXT?!
I can't take this shit any more, SO JUST GET ME THE FUCK OUT!!!

Insects Inside

I can feel them crawling, up and down my spine.
I can feel them moving, right behind my eyes.
I can feel it burning, as they wait beneath my flesh.
So I try to cut them out, but they're just too fast.

I know that I'm a dead man, awake in his grave.
I know that I am falling, a million miles away from sane.
I can feel as they are eating, me from the inside to the out.
I can feel them crawling, and I know that they want out...

I think that I can be forgiven, someday when I am gone.
In the end, it might have been a sin but I know I wasn't wrong.
I can feel them crawling, all the insects inside my head.
I know that I am a dead man, still waiting on his death.
"And I know I'm almost there..."

Wrath Has Spoken

Mother was calling, now it is time to go home.
The hours are falling, now our hearts become stone.
This hurt is still growing, as my body becomes weak.
Why am I still here crying, just praying for release.

For I am nothing to you, just a waste of your time.
I am not a great person, I'm not even human most times.
I am only a nonentity, trying to be a little more.
I am a fragmented memory, hidden behind that open door.

Wrath has spoken, and now it is come to be that time.
The end has come again, and we've been waiting for awhile.
As time is constant draining, falling straight through the cracks.
The end it has come, and we are all now but only ash.

Mother was waiting, for us to come home that day.
But we must have gotten lost, out deep in the rain.
With pain and hatred still growing, we just can't save us.
Wrath had then spoken, and then our world just burned away.

They Told You

Let now the razor sink.
Wake now in dire dreams.
Frozen in fear of what comes next.
Then salvation is found.
Hidden underneath the stitch.

Tilt then the candle and pour the wax.
Over these eyes to hide what is next.
So do just as they told you.
Bury me under all the dead fallen leaves.
Shift then the rusted razor.
To awake here in my dire dreams.

"You cannot save me..."

Follow the Intentions

Down a long hall, she leads me to the back.
Her voice is very quiet, but her eyes said a lot.
So I followed her intentions, all the way to the stars.
And still to this day, I can remember her touch.

She was leading me, into the pleasures of bliss.
She told me to let go, to enjoy the ride and release my breath.
I wanted to save us, from not ending that way.
She looked deep into my eyes, then said it will all be okay.

I'll always remember, when she led me to the back room.
I'll always remember, how great it felt as she kissed my neck.
She told me to follow, all the way until only peace remains.
All of her intentions were great, but it was time that slipped away.

Into a better dimension, where we could be together always.
She was so great to me, and I don't think that I deserved it.
She just wanted me to follow, and to feel the glory of pure bliss.
Still to this day I can remember the taste, of our very last kiss...

Drilling Into the Spine

Into the morning it goes screaming.
Left for dead, just fucked and bleeding.
Where does the all the pain go in the end?
"PLEASE JUST GET ME OUT OF MY HEAD TODAY!!!"

On goes the drilling, into this spine to erase the past.
The drugs are trying to numb it down, but they never seem to last.
As then to be, of that perverted truth left screaming.
"PLEASE JUST GET ME OUT OF MY HEAD!!!"

On and on into the morning goes the screaming.
I was left for dead, just fucked and bleeding.
Where does all of the pain go to in the end?
"PLESAE JUST GET ME THE FUCK OUT OF MY OWN HEAD!!!"

Faces Watching Over

Within the abyss I've been for so very many ages.
Decades filling the hourglass, now nearing an ending.
Those faces have been watching over for ages.
Looking inside of this tormented poet's mind.

I wish that there could be a chance for me to save us.
But we are all damned and have been sense the beginning.
And even then, those faces have been watching over.
Trying to understand why it is that we're all dead.

Within the abyss I've been for so many ages.
I wish that there would have been at lest a change to save us.
But we are only, to be at the edge for so many ages.
The faces tear inside, and only death they could see...

Into Madness

Into the madness I am screaming.
All in my dreams, dead and weeping.
A voice in my heart that desires.
A chance to see beyond this rage.

For now but only to let fall.
And we know now that the future is yesterday.
And here I go screaming into madness once again.
"Just tell me that I'll be okay!!!"

As I am falling into madness.
I have to say that reality was a fun trip indeed.
Still in my head the voices ring.
Hoping for a chance to feel something beyond rage...

In the End (All Fades Away.)

Take us back to a time when we were together.
A time when we were youthful and ready for the day.
Take us back to a time, when our only dream was a family.
A time when we wanted only to hold each other *forever and a day.*

As into the outlandish memories of a time gone.
Remember the lyrics if you can and try to sing along.
The story has changed now and there is no going back.
We have now only, the truth of our twisted ends.

We tried our best but in the end all faded away.
We wanted to love forever, but then all became cold that day.
As now there is nothing left, only the truth of our dead souls.
We could not change it, the death of our beautiful dreams.

Take us back to a time when we were happy together.
A time when we were so deeply in love and held each other all day.
Take us back to that moment, when we knew that we had so much more time.
Time to love each other before it all just fades away...

What Does It Make of Me?

I have murdered, so what does that make of me?
I am a sinner, a monster that hides in your every dream.
I have over the years destroyed so many lives.
So tell me now, what does this make of me?

I have tried to be a hero, there to save the day.
I have been the victim, when they all threw me away.
I have killed so many, of innocent lives over the years.
So tell me now, what does this make of me!?

I have seen the ending, but I will never tell.
I know how the story will change, so many more times.
I will be the monster, hiding forever in your every dream.
So just tell me now, what does all of this make of me!!?

Variety of Fatalities

Over the line and spoken more than needed.
Left at a fork in the road and it's so very uneasy.
We're ready for some change now, something more than this.
We are ready for something new now, *"a much better death."*

Over the line now and left behind the rhyme.
We have reached a fork in the road and we're running out of time.
We are ready to change this, to find some much better way.
To find a new way of ending this fucked up page.

Equidistant

Time to just fucking do it, and admit to what I am.
I've been doing this for ages, fighting these endless wars.
But it might someday be over, and then we'll find peace.
We're almost out now, just push a little more to ease the pain.

Over years of weeping acid tears out of my eyes.
Years of cutting at my flesh, just to pass some time.
Ages upon ages of reaching into the darkness so blind.
We're almost out now, just a few more lines.

Time to just say fuck it and admit that I am a monster.
I truly am but a demon with angel wings.
But we might reach an end someday, and we'll then be at peace.
"We're not even halfway through yet - I say..."

It's almost over, and then the credits can roll.
We've been trying our best, to end these wars of our minds.
But we're still far from an ending, we just need to give it some time.
We're about halfway through now, and soon to honor our pride.

Cigarettes Burning

Stale smoke lingering, upon the tips of my taste buds.
The burn of the whiskey reminds me, of all in which I have done.
Out here in this field I am screaming, but she cannot hear.
As at the end of this rope I have been swinging, for so very many years.

The cigarettes are burning, flooding my lungs with ash.
The whiskey is consuming me, because I no longer want to look back.
Out here in this field I am tripping, but she can no longer hear.
At the end of this rope I've been swinging, *just swimming through her hair.*

Stale smoke still lingering, upon the edge of this rusted blade.
The burn of the whiskey soothed by the marijuana, *so I begin to feel okay.*
Out here in this field I've been tripping, deep into the unknown.
At the end of this rope I've been waiting, *for the sun to melt away the snow.*

The cigarettes are burning, now I'm smoking only ash.
The whiskey is burning, boiling hatred within my chest.
Out here in this field I am alone, but she cannot hear.
At the end of this rope I've been swinging, *still swimming through her hair.*

Until the Rain Dries

Someday I do plan on returning to my mind.
Someday I do hope for us to see beyond the night.
Into dreams all shall venture in grace.
Someday I do plan on waking to see, what has become of me.

With these jagged thorns growing from beneath my flesh.
I feel such pain now, as God puts his hand on my chest.
But I cannot return until all the rain dries.
Our world is flooding, and we all just drift aside.

I do someday plan on returning back to my mind.
This has been a long trip, and has been quite some time.
Into dreams we all did venture, into a world of grace.
Someday I do plan on waking, when all the blood just dries away.

To Prove Myself

Truth be told, I did this all just to prove myself.
I have fought these wars, here upon all levels of hell.
I have died a million deaths, and millions more to come.
Miles upon miles still ahead, and not over until it's done.

So truth be told, I did this all only to prove myself.
A dead poet, describing his oh so very beautiful hells.
I have died a million deaths, only for me to feel alive.
I did this to prove myself, my beautiful poetic wastes of time.

I did this all to prove to you, I am more than just a sideshow freak.
I chose to fight all these wars, just to prove that I'm not weak.
I have died a million deaths, and still millions more yet to be.
I did this to prove to myself, I truly am, *"the demon with angel wings."*

Bitter Whispers

Bitter whispers stuck in the hive that is my brain.
A broken fragmented thought, reminding me I am insane.
This flesh is soft now, and tastes so familiar.
Screams echoing on into the night, felt now as only bitter whispers.

The moon is falling now, and mother-earth begins to weep.
The shepherd cannot protect us, his so very pathetic little sheep.
The gods all laugh together, at the sights of our dismay.
This flesh tastes so familiar, because I am eating my own face.

The earthworms are altogether thriving, living in my veins.
A broken fragmented soul, decaying here in my grave.
This flesh is so delicious, and reminds me of the past.
Screams echoing on through the night, just bitter whispers in my head.

Her Eyes So Cold

Her eyes so cold, groping around within my heart.
My death so cold, as by angels I was torn apart.
Our universe is ending now, soon only an empty void.
Her eyes so cold, holding me now beyond the grave.

Her voice was soothing, it lives on still within me.
I have burned for my sins, and I will never forgive me.
No justifying the ends, only pointless bloodshed and death.
I shall never be forgiven, not after what I did.

Her eyes so cold, groping around within my heart.
So damn funny, that by angels I was torn apart.
Our universe is ending, and we just cannot see.
Her eyes so cold, burning forever within me.

I Haven't Tried

I haven't tried to kill myself.
Because I already know I can.
I haven't tried to say I love you.
Even though I know I can't.
I haven't tried to reach out.
Because I know no one cares.
I haven't tried to speak to God.
Because I know he cannot hear.
I haven't tried to take your life.
Because I already know that I can.
I have never tried to say that I'm sorry.
But I promise I will.
Upon another rant.

Ghosts Are Reaching

Ghosts are reaching into my brain.
Death has spoken his poison into these veins.
The Devil he asks me, how do I feel?
Never better my friend, now smile as we fade.

Ghosts are reaching into my thoughts.
Driving me into tormenting fears and shock.
The Devil he questions, if we were ever truly real.
As our realities bleed out, of these wounds that cannot heal.

Sanity is gone now, as it always has been.
Death has spoken, his needle into my spine.
So we all begin to question, if we were ever truly alive.
As all the ghosts are reaching, and taking away our lives.

Pain still holds it together, reminding us why.
Death is truly dead now, "guess he ran out of time."
These drugs keep us moving, far beyond our graves.
The ghosts are reaching in, as we all try to fade away.

Our Past Is Dead

Our past is dead and it's my fault.
Our future is pointless, and it's still my fault.
All hope is dead now, buried in our graves.
Sanity then whispers, a bullet into our brains.

Scream with me, the lyrics of Evil & Pain...
Die with me, and let us fuck this life insane.
Remember me, when the story comes to an end.
Let me go, to spare yourself some pain.

Our past is dead and it's all my fault.
Our future is fucked and it's still my fault.
Our world is dead now, pages burnt to ash.
So we weep for the death, of both our future and our past.

Weeping Razors

Weeping rusted razors from my eyes.
Because I know truly, soon I'm gonna die.
So try to hold on, to me while you can.
Forget me now, then just walk away.

I am regurgitating bloody tar, into this paper sheet.
I am remembering now, the bliss of pure insanity.
So try to hold onto me, before we all slip away.
Forget me while you can, "Please just walk away."

Weeping rusted razor blades from my eyes.
Bleeding out all of the pills, I have consumed over time.
My eyes roll back, and I look then at my brain.
So I just forget myself, and then I walk away.

Establishing Supremacy

Unlock and open these doors, before I break them down.
Unsay what you have spoken, and fucking do it now.
Listen and pay attention, because I will not repeat myself.
Do as you are told, and you better fucking do it now!

My hands around your throat, and I stare into your eyes.
Lingering tastes of a burnt clove, echoing down my spine.
Of our truths, in blood they soak, now tasting so very ripe.
Just fucking do as I tell you, and turn off these fucking lights.

Aim now at my forehead, and pull the trigger tight.
Laugh at the explosion of sanity, and I guess we were right.
Do now as I tell you, and eat that which made me, Me.
Taste my insanity, and now I guess, "You are me."

Laughing here, in complete control.

Chapter 8

Psychosomatically

Glass Pipe

Speak now with the voices behind my eyes.
Drive the needle in, and then load the pipe.
Fuck yesterday and the tomorrows before it.
Lift now this page and then just fucking burn it.

I was just a mistake, bringing forth destruction.
I am an act of God, posing as the Devil.
I am a sweet voice, kissing upon your lips.
I am burning within this pipe, such a delicious fragrance as we kiss.

Speak now with the voices, that wait behind my eyes.
Look into the shadow, beyond both space and time.
Our lives were truly pointless, as we still remain today.
Broken then the glass pipe, and of the shards we eat.

I was just a nonsense, beginning to make some sense.
I am an act of God, I am your immortal sins.
So fuck yesterday, and every tomorrow before it.
Roll up this page, and let us now just burn it.

Respect Driven

Only receiving that which was given.
Lies go unspoken and still respect driven.
As all my cells they whisper, we have gone away.
Pain is now a pleasure, and it feels so fucking great.

Our minds are fucking breaking, here at the bottom of this pit.
Our love will someday save us, "*but I'm full of shit.*"
Our words go on unspoken, felt both pride and shame.
Still by respect am driven, far beyond the grave.

Only to receive that which was once given.
Of our deaths go now unspoken, and still so very unseen.
All of what I am is lost now, deep under the sea.
Pain is my greatest pleasure, and it feels fucking great.

Lock Us In (*I Could Sin.*)

From the dead speakers, a voice begins to rise.
It might be a ghost, or just the voices in my mind.
This house it could be haunted, or maybe it's me.
From the dead speakers the voices rise, and this is what they say...

Lock us in, I could sin and it would all be the same.
Lock us in, I could sin as here in my grave.
Lock us in, in no light as for ages we shall fight.
Lock us in, deep within so we shall remain the same.

From the dead speakers, a haunting voice spoke to me.
It might have been a ghost, or maybe it was just me.
This house is surely haunted, as is my broken mind.
From the dead speakers the voice had risen, and it said one more time...

"Lock us in, I could sin."

Laid In the Sun

A rotting carcass laid in the sun.
A laughing bastard loading his gun.
A twisted nature of growing shame.
Endless chatter spewing from under the page.
Devils screaming as they turn to salt.
Our whole world is now ending.
And truth be told it was my fault.
As a rotting carcass laid in the sun.
Remembers the truth of what we've done.
Still the bastard he laughs and loads his gun.
With more mindless nonsense filling this hollow grave.
God is dead now and it's my fault.
So we all weep and turn to salt.
As the bastard is laughing remembering how great it tastes.
The carcass of the Devil laid in the sun.
And like death and tar.
It tastes so great...

140

Things I Put Up With

The sands of time eating away at my sanity.
Where have I been all this time?
Locked in a box, no air holes to breathe.
Things I put up with, in this fucked up reality.

And it's such a bitter tragedy, left all alone to just fucking bleed.
It's such a bitter tragedy, the fact that we were all just fucked away.
These are the things that I put up with, upon every day.
Someone please just get me out, of this fucked up reality.

The sands of time all covering me.
I am now a statue of a dead poet, honored for his pains.
Remember all you can of the truth, that we are one and the same.
These are things I put up with, upon every fucking day.

And yes it's such a tragedy, so here alone I just weep and bleed.
Such a twisted tragedy, the fact that we were all just fucked away.
These are things I wish I could just let be.
Fucked up things I have to put up with, every fucking day.

Busy Days

This acid tastes like a forgotten part of me.
Truth be told, my poems don't remember what to say.
But still I'm left upon these crowded streets.
Moving onward into these endless busy days.

Now can you reach in and tear out that greatest part of me.
The man you wish to respect someday.
Look back and try to remember me, I am the one that got away.
Still onward moving upon these crowded streets, endless busy days.

And there goes all of my sanity, spread out upon the page.
My love what now has become of me, *I guess I am the monster you hate.*
Still I roam and stalk upon these crowded streets.
Moving onward as I feast, endless upon these busy days.

Call To the Never

Trust forsaken, and we never had a chance.
Hope was lost and forgotten, so we never looked back.
My hatred it was consuming, every last little bit of me.
So on I go screaming, here below the sea.

Upon all levels of existence I've been tripping.
Trying to learn the one undeniable truth of the fact.
As I called into the Never, and I never heard back.
Still on goes the tripping, and I can never go back...

I'm so fucking sick, I think I'm dying.
Or maybe I'm just having a fucked up fit.
The room looks like its melting.
What the fuck could have done all of this.!?

As trust was forsaken, and we never did have a chance.
Hope was truly forgotten, so we never looked back.
My hatred it consumed me, and still it does to this day.
So on and on I call to the never, waiting to hear what it will have to say.

On Dark-Wings

Death brought upon dark wings.
Come to just take us away.
Pain is all that's left in my heart today.
"God I want a second chance!"

As such a twisted nature did birth.
The true end of our world to be.
I am the answer to the question.
Brought upon dark wings.

With sanity to guide the way.
And what have the Gods now to say?
Of the ending that has come to be.
Set forth upon, these dark wings...

She Shattered

She shattered into pieces, with porcelain-doll screams.
Fuck inebriations, and all your vain dreams.
Let us speak now of the honor, to fight this war together.
And pride shall be discovered, between flesh and bone....

She shattered into pieces, as did all my memories of then.
We wanted to be together forever, but it all ended upon that sin.
So let us speak now of the reason, as to why we are still here.
Hold on as tight as you can my love, before we all just fade away.

She shattered into pieces, the great love of my past.
She was all I ever wanted, and Fate just took her back.
I guess that I wasn't ready, to feel true love at that time.
She was all I ever wanted, but then she just died...

She shattered into pieces, as did my heart on that day.
Fuck inebriations, and all these fucking games.
Let us speak now of the answers, to all our questions unasked.
As she did shatter, I had died with her and I wish never to come back.

Cut the Roots Out

Cut out the roots of the thorn vines, that grows beneath my flesh.
Cut out the roots of the sickness, the heart inside my chest.
Take me back the beginning, before our love had failed.
So I can let you kill me, to prevent what I have done.

Cut out the roots of the thorn vines, that grows beneath my flesh.
Cut out the roots of my past now, so what have I left?
Take me to the end of my sanity, so I can feel okay.
Cut out the roots of my soul now, so I can fade away.

Beyond this world of torment, that eats at my mind.
Beyond this endless torment, dripping down my spine.
Just cut out all the reasons, so we'll have nothing to say.
Cut out the roots of my being, straight from my brain...

Upon Speculation

Upon speculation of my tattered soul.
Truly I know I'm just a fucking disease.
A cancer growing within a man's soul.
I am the answer to the demon's dreams.

So rise now and fall with me.
Let us go tripping within the clouds of smoke.
And soon enough all will taste as but a dream.
As we dance endlessly within the smoke.

Upon speculation of my demonic heart.
Truly I know now I am just a fucking disease.
A cancer growing upon our souls.
I am the rising nightmare within the demon's dreams.

So laugh with me as we fall my love.
Only to see how deep is this hole.
And soon enough we will come to be.
Laughing endless in our smoke filled graves.

Doctors Hacking At Me

My eyes are stitched shut, so I cannot see.
As these hell driven doctors, start hacking at me.
They are trying to cut out, my immortal soul.
But they can find nothing, but a heart made of coal.

My arms and legs have been sawed off.
My mouth sewn shut, so I cannot scream.
On and on these hell driven doctors, continue to hack at me.
Because they enjoy watching me in pain.

I just gotta get the fuck out!
I need to get the fuck out!
God just get me the fuck out!
Out of this world of pain...

With Another Breath

Raining cocaine and sweet twisted nonsense.
Heroin pumping through these veins.
As the razors cut at me so very violent.
I cannot seem to erase this page.
With another breath, I break the silence.

Raining acid and flooding my grave.
The picture on the wall, now it's fucking burning.
As we watch the true death of my soul.
I have to laugh because I deserve it.
And just another breath, as here I lie burning.

No second chance, it's one shot in a million.
Cocaine driving my conscience, as does the heroin.
I cannot end this torment, because I enjoy how it tastes.
As I scream out all the razors, filling an empty page.
With another breath I'll explain it, what all of this means...

First Love / No Chance

God give me the motivation for another rant.
Erase all memories of me, if you can.
Cut into the center of this, then close your eyes.
First love had no chance, so it just died.

As ancient spirits are weeping, have we any right.
As our pasts have been fleeting, our entire lives.
There is nothing left but insanity, only that and pain.
God please kill all memories, that remain of me.

Forget me now if you have the chance, I am just a waste of time.
God help me end this pointless rant, echoing in my mind.
Cut deep into the center of me, rip out my poetic heart.
Our first love had no chance, so it was just torn apart.

Particles Of Platinum Teardrops

Atomic bombs filling the sky today, raining nuclear screams.
All matter that once made us real, it was then raped away.
As particles of platinum teardrops, they sank into our flesh.
We had not even a second, until we became but ash.

The skies are turning black now, but I believe it is noon.
Our atoms were all broken away, bringing forth our doom.
We had not even a chance to say, that we're sorry for our sins.
Before the particles of platinum teardrops, they took us all away.

Atomic bombs filled the skies earlier today, *but now the clouds are on fire.*
All matter and existence was raped away, and still to this day we are burning.
So we had nothing to say, before our flesh became but ash.
As all the particles of platinum teardrops, came to take us away.

Eating Weed

All is calm and so very silent.
The notion is called and we're out of time again.
The Darkness calls, it wants us to return again.
So all is calm, here in hell so very silent.

I'm eating weed, just so I can really feel it.
I'm drinking the poison, but at least I can admit it.
I am feeling quite strange now, can't fully describe it.
I've been eating the weed, and you should really try this...

For all is calm now and so very silent.
The notions are numbed out and they all do rhyme again.
The Darkness is calling, it wants to feast on us again.
I eat all the weed, so everything is very calm and silent.

Then Goes Silent

The trigger pulled, and then all goes silent.
She kissed my lips, then all went blind again.
We took a chance then, but sadly we failed.
The candles all burnt out, and all is silent.

For hours it is falling, the memory of back then.
The dreams of her remind me, I am but a sin.
All truth of the matter is burned away, lost with all the ash.
Then goes silent with all the pain, "Oh an ending at last..."

The trigger pulled, and I am dead again.
I'm just a shallow fool, remembering how blind I am.
Our love it was so fucking great back then.
When all was at peace, tranquil and very quiet.

As for hours it was screaming, the voice inside my brain.
The dreams were all dying, so I guess nothing changed.
We took a chance at loving again, only to feel more pain.
Then goes silent, all of the demons within my veins.

SkunkBaby

Out on display, since the first day.
The sideshow freak, inside the glass cage.
They all look inside, to see the creature.
The monster born to destroy our lives.

Laugh all together at the little freak of nature.
Point your fingers as I break down and cry.
Laugh it up all together while you can.
Because soon enough you're gonna die.

I was out on display, since my first day.
I was born as nothing more than a sideshow freak.
Why did all just point and laugh.
At the freak, known as "Me"...

Living On Death

Been living on death all my life.
Been beating my head, but all in spite.
Been fighting this torment all of my days.
Been lost for so long, within this maze.

Still hoping for reason, beyond all the chaos.
Still frozen in time, forgotten and surely lost.
Still fighting the torments, of being insane.
Still I have only my madness, to keep we awake.

Been living on death for all of my life.
Been beating my head, but all just in spite.
Been dying to live now, and see tomorrow fade.
Been so long since I could tell you, "Just get the fuck away!"

Still hoping for a reply, from the God in the sky.
Still staring up at the sun, until we all go blind.
Still fighting all the chaos, that makes me, "Me".
Still I know the truth, that we were never free.

"Living on death, and still dying to dream..."

Distorted Blood-Flow

It sounds like thunder, falling from the sky.
It looks like the Devil, might have changed his mind.
It feels like we're burning, here in this cold.
It's time now to end us, God take our souls.

Pushing further upon the distorted blood flow.
Truthfully I feel like I'm gonna die.
But worry not yourself my love.
Because I know, it is now my time.

"Forgive me..."

Demons Of God

Follow the demise of faith and the birth of loss.
Led six feet deep into our graves, cold and covered in frost.
We are the forgotten, the children that were lost.
We are the demons, the demons of your God.

Listen to the reverbs, soothing these twisted manners.
Hold onto my heart now, and sing along with the chorus.
We are led into our madness, but it was all just a lie.
We are the demons, the creatures that can never see the light.

Follow the demise of faith and the birth of true loss.
We are led beyond our graves, frozen and covered in frost.
We have always been the forgotten, children of the lost.
We are the one true mistake, we are the demons of God.

This Mask Broken

This mask broken, exposing my true face.
The riddle now remembered, so what have you to say?
This flesh it is decaying, yet I am still alive.
We are all in pieces, praying to see another night.

This mask is broken, as is my tattered face.
The riddle it makes sense now, if you remember what they say.
The questions are all a miss now, as is our tired souls.
This mask it is broken, so now I'm all alone.

Our live have been destroyed, from the very beginning.
We were just too young, to understand the ending.
This flesh it is decaying, even though I am still alive.
This mask broken, exposing you to my fucked up life.

In Art Remembered

The truth of me, it lies in splinters.
The death of love, upon that dreaded winter.
In one swift move, it was all remembered.
The artwork known, as all of *our burnt pictures.*

In death is honored, truly cherished.
In life was forgotten, pushed as so fucking pointless!
In art remembered, the fact of the Devil I am.
The picture remains, stained with blood and sins.

The truth of me, it is scattered about in fucking splinters.
The death of our love, it goes on so very cherished.
Then in one swift move, everything was forgotten.
All of the artworks, known as our beautiful souls.

Happy Birthday (*My Lovely Dreams.*)

Thousands of strange planets orbiting about in space.
The hands of an alien God, stretching across the entire galaxy.
The laws of reality are gone, so life is as a dream.
Then we all go on tripping, into the bliss of a silent night.

Millions of stars dancing about, and dying out in space.
On my body are endless amounts of scars, so that is my fate.
So happy birthday my lovely dreams, and welcome back again.
We've been gone for so long, but we never truly left...

There are thousands of strange planets, dead here in space.
Still they orbit about, waiting for their chance to fade.
We just want to leave now, and end all of these pains.
And as we begin to decay, I remember that this is just a dream...

For Sweet Nothings

My head below the waves, now I can see it.
All in life so dire and grim, "no, you cannot free it."
For sweet nothings it is remembered, still so very cherished.
So please let us fade, to the other side of our sanities.

My head below the waves, so I could meet death and see it.
As my life flashed before my eyes, I began to miss it.
There was so many reasons, for me to stand up and fight.
So many sweet nothings, that got me through those nights...

Fuck The Next Page

Fuck the next page, and every one before it.
Fuck you and your faith, because it gets us nowhere.
Fuck all of this inside my head, causing so much torment.
Fuck the next page, and all the thousands before it...

Fuck this dead-earth we made, now we cannot save it.
Fuck all the shit they say, because it's all the same again.
Fuck this Goddamn world, and everybody in it.
Fuck the next page, and all the thousands to follow it...

Gambling Away My Soul

It's come down to this, I'm gambling away my soul.
It's time to shift the wrist, now our bodies growing cold.
There is no time to waste, so we just enjoy it.
Yes, come and follow me, deep into the graveyard.

It's come down to this, I'm gambling away my worthless soul.
I've run out of luck, now everything is growing cold.
There is no time left, for either of us to save this.
So the card is drawn, and we just cannot change it...

You Have No Say

You have no say, in how I end this.
I've had no say, from the very beginning.
You have no say, in how I kill you.
I've had no say, and will never have any...

You have no hope left, your world is ending.
And you've had no say, since the very begingnig.
You have no say, so don't try to change it.
I have no say - in how I will end this...

Disclosure

Time has come, for us to say.
It's been a fun trip, into our graves.
Time has come, for us to say.
That nothing in this world will ever fully change.

The lies are failing, we are learning the truth.
The end is coming, and it's all because of me and you.
Our lives were taken, and all of them just fucked away.
It's time the world knew, what it is that we have to say...

Reading Me...

All of this time, you've been reading me like a book.
All of this time, I was just a turning page.
All of my life, I have lived in pain and shame.
All of us are dying, now just burning away.

You've been reading me, like I was a book.
You've been reading me, to learn what it took.
You've been watching me, to see how I die.
You've been reading me, but I think you skipped a line...

Chapter 9

At the Epicenter

Encroaching

At a place, where I know I should not be.
Roaming the vast pits of hell, on my own so very lonely.
The Devil he whispers, logic into our hearts.
God he encourages us, to reach beyond the stars.

I'm at a place now, where I know that I should not be.
Wandering the abysses of hell, with no one beside me.
I guess I deserve this, all of the pain I have endured.
God please just wake me now, so I can go to sleep...

I'm at a place right now, a place where I know I should not be.
I am lost out here, in the vast wastelands of hell.
The Devil is trying to find me, but up to now he has failed.
So God just watches, as I wander lost for an eternity.

Secluded Memories

Someone out there is getting the best of me.
Still I try to keep, as least one secluded memory.
Something that is mine, and for no one else.
And I shall hold that memory, forever here in hell.

Someone out there is getting the very best of me.
Still I try to shake it off, the thought of what has happened to me.
Something has gone wrong, at some point or another.
All of my memories are gone now, seeping into the pages.

Someone out there has gotten the very best of me.
Still I try to fight it, just to keep one little part of me.
Something that is mine, a forgotten secluded memory.
And I shall hold onto it, forever here in hell where I will stay.

That House In the Woods

I can remember that house in the woods.
I felt so at peace, as I roamed through its halls.
I can remember that house in the woods.
That beautiful place that I call home.

That house in the woods, it is the greatest part of me.
That house in the woods, hidden within all the trees.
That house in the woods, I wish to return there.
That house in the woods, the only place I know I am free.

I can remember, when she kissed my lips that day.
It felt so great, but hurt when she had walked away.
Then all became so darkened, numbed down in my heart.
So I return to that house in the woods, the place I call home...

Ensuring Victory

Ensuring victory, by rigging the game.
Taking out all the other opponents.
Doing truly what ever it takes.
Ensuring our victory, by fixing the game.

We've come too far, to just turn back right now.
We've gotten so high, now above the clouds.
We've done what we needed to, to ensure our victory.
We've taken care of it all, so just enjoy the games.

Ensuring victory, by doing what it takes.
Kill all, of whom ever stands in my way.
Doing everything, to ensure that we win.
Victory shall be ours, because there is no turning back.

Mysterious Visions

Mysterious visions imprinted into my brain.
Voices of my dead loves, ringing on within my ear today.
It's almost time to just let go and fall asleep.
But the visions still haunt me, and they won't go away.

Mysterious visions plaguing me into my grave.
Memories of a forgotten time, when we were ready for the day.
It is almost time now, for us to let go and fade away.
But these visions, they can't remain forever in my brain.

Come and let us fall now, upon the other side.
Come let us dream now, before we open our eyes.
Come let us scream now, just so we can get it out.
Come and let us see now, the darkness in the light.

Mysterious visions imprinted into my brain.
Lingering voices of my dead loves, reminding me to stay.
It's almost time now, for us to let go and just fall asleep.
But still her whispers haunt me, and they won't go away.

Results of Abuse

This broken body is the result of years of abuse.
This tired mind is reaching, put only pulling back ash.
The hourglass is broken, spilling out all of its sands.
So we're running out of time, and it's not coming back.

This broken body is the greatest proof, that it is fucking hell.
This twisted mind should have proven by now.
That none of these endless wounds can ever heal.
These are the results of abuse, and how for you it will feel.

This broken body, its falling down and it can't get up.
This twisted mind, it is dead now and was always fucked.
The hourglass it is broken, so I guess we ran out of time.
It's never coming back, so again I'm abused to an inch of my life.

Eclectic

A decade of ranting and raving upon my endless battles.
I am a man of many voices, and everyday it changes.
It's been so very long now, since this whole thing started.
Decades of ranting and raving, endless about all my dreams.

I have been fighting, so many different wars.
I have been dying, so many brutal deaths.
I have been screaming, but no one seems to hear.
I have been weeping, and no one ever cared.

It's been quite some time now, decades come and gone.
I am a man of many different battles, and they all still move on.
It's been so very long now, since this whole thing began.
Decades I have been doing this, moving onward upon another rant.

I have been frying, baked to the core and I feel like shit.
I think I am dying, and I know that I am fucking sick!
I have been dreaming, that someday we would again meet.
I have been so many different things, and all of them are truly me...

The Owl Watches

The owl watches, as I cut my flesh away.
The demons are weeping, because they didn't get their way.
The owl it is watching, just choosing its time.
The angels are all screaming, because now it is time.

The owl it is calling, to my dying soul.
The Devil he his calling, but I had to put him on hold.
Because me and God were talking, about the end of time.
The owl is just waiting, to have a taste of mine...

The insects are all growing, beneath my rotten flesh.
The ghosts are all weak now, I guess they have nothing left.
The end it is coming, but sadly not today.
The owl it watches, and on and on it will wait...

Needles to Comfort

In go the weeping needles, to comfort my fragile mind.
On goes the tormenting hatred, time after time.
Pain holds me in check still, to this very day.
In go all the weeping needles, trying to keep me sane.

We reach beyond these pages, to touch the hearts of many.
Together we are one, within ourselves we are so many.
We've all come undone, and we could not change that.
The pain it just goes on, and nothing can ever stop it.

As in go the needles, to comfort my shattered mind.
On goes the drugging, of my body and my time.
We are all falling into pieces, and are never to be fixed.
So the needles they inject, right into my wrist.

We have all reached beyond it, this torn up bloody page.
Together we are one, but we never can be again.
We've died to prove that we will, be the ones to say.
The needles are here to comfort me, from all of the endless pain.

Objectives Meeting

My mouth is bleeding.
My eyes are weeping.
My heart is screaming.
My God he is dreaming.
My hatred is growing.
My death it is showing.
Red ice it is snowing.
Inside I can no longer hold this.
The conclusion it is coming.
The streets they are burning.
My mouth it is bleeding.
But I am proud to know.
All my objectives are being met...

Aged Murder

How long have I been weeping over her murder?
How many years now have I been fighting to breathe?
How much longer until I can escape this?
How many more years before I can set my soul free?

It is falling onto the concrete, it is spelling out "Rage".
It has been so many years now, here in this blood filled grave.
It is going to be a while, before I'm able to return again.
It is time for me to let go, and take control once again.

How long have we been fighting over the fact of her murder?
How many years have I been weeping, over her grave?
How many more times must I say it, before someone understands?
How truly aged is the murder, of our mortal whims?

It is falling into the ground now, soon to be all away.
It has been so very long now, thousands and thousands of pains.
It is going to be alright, we just need to find release.
It is going to be okay I say, so let us all just fade away...

Time Is Ticking Away

Reveries of our laughter, and in time it all fades.
Revenge of the monster, and I shall have my day...
Reunited with my hatred, and now I feel whole.
Returning to hell now, so I can take back my soul.

Time is constant fading, ticking and slipping away.
Death is now so pleasant, with blood rubbed in my face.
Time is constantly dying, as are we all each and everyday.
Time it is slipping, time is constantly ticking away.

Hoping of some greater nonsense, found in my heart.
Heeding what was told to me, from the very start.
Heading into darkness, because that is all I've ever known.
Hearing the constant ticking, as time it just fades away...

160

Pull Me Closer

Pull me in closer until our flesh fuses together.
Love me forever and on and on some more.
Tell me that I was your hero, tell that I meant to you, more.
Pull me closer until we are one, forever to be in love.

Tell me that I am a dreamer, and that I need to awake.
Tell me that I'm worthless, just a fucking waste.
Tell me that you hate me, and I guess it's all the same.
Tell me that I'm dead right now, *then pull me closer and throw me away.*

Love me for never, and there was a time when I cared.
Tell me that I'm a bastard, and you know I never was there.
Pull me in much closer, until we become one.
Tell me that I am nothing, but God's greatest mistake.

Pull me in closer until our flesh fuses together.
Cut me out of yourself, because there is no other way.
Tell me that I'm a dreamer, then let me get some sleep.
Wake me at the ending, although it has already passed...

Gravitate to Me

Look into my eyes and see.
Reach into my heart to know.
Speak into my mind to embrace.
Kiss me upon the lips.
Then we burn away.

Screaming into my heart with rage.
Reach behind my eyes to feel.
Look into my soul to cherish.
The fact of this broken heart.
In which can never heal.

"Just gravitate to me my love..."

My Advice

My advice to you, would be to just smile and scream.
I know that sounds stupid, but you've gotta trust me.
My heart it has been out there, wandering through the graveyards.
I know you might not understand, but you just need to trust me.

My advice to you, would be to just let it all go.
Remember that you are not alone, out here in this poetic battlefield.
I know that it's hard to understand, all the bullshit I say.
But you just need to trust me, because it will all be okay.

My advice to you, would be to never stop fighting for your children.
I know you will be strong, and do whatever you can to defend them.
My heart has been out there, to feel the pain of being torn apart.
I know you might not understand me, but please take my advice...

"Smile and scream..."

Ripen In the Dawn

Watch as the carcass ripens at the dawn.
Weep at the foot of the demon.
Just try your best to remember our song.
Just leave while you can, *"but you ran out of time..."*

Watch as our destinies, begin to ripen at the dawn.
Weep as we are burned at the stake, yet nothing we have done.
Just try to look away, as our ending begins to near.
Just try to let go and enjoy all the pain.

Laugh with me my love, at the truth of our time.
Look into the future I say, you see we're out of time.
Watch as the end shall ripen, there at the dawn.
Just try your very best my love, to just sing along.

Little Angels Burning

The little angels wandered too far into the abyss.
Now they are lost, and sadly will be missed.
The little angels were seeking, an audience with the Devil.
Sadly in the end, that is in fact what they got.

The little angels were weeping, because they had surely lost their way.
The Devil had only laughed and then cast them away.
The little angels all questioned, if they will ever again see the light.
The Devil just smiled, and then vanished before their eyes.

The little angels were curious, of what they'd find in the pit.
They knew not to venture there, but they sadly did.
All the little angels, they are afraid now and want to go home.
But they can see only darkness, and the dying of all hope.

The little angels were brave, they knew what they were up against.
But they had to see for themselves, what was hiding in the pit.
The little angels, their greatest dreams were of learning.
As for now in hell, they are forever burning...

Attacking My Reflections

My fist strikes at the mirror.
Because of what my reflection had said.
I begin to smash my head against the mirror.
Because I want that motherfucker dead.

I am attacking my reflection, because I know he is evil.
I am trying to save myself, from becoming a fucking demon.
I have tried to be more, than a murderer of my own dreams.
I am attacking my reflection, because of what he said to me.

My fist cracks against the mirror.
Because of what my reflection had said.
So I take that damn mirror, and smash it against my head.
All because I want that motherfucker dead...!

Drive Us to Wonder

Drive us to wonder, why we are still here.
Lead us to heaven, lead us beyond fear.
Drive us to wonder, of the answers they hide.
Lead us to heaven, help us to open our eyes.

Drive us to wonder, why we are bleeding still.
Lead us to question, why our wounds cannot heal.
Drive us to wonder, why it is we stayed.
Lead us to heaven, and at peace we shall stay.

Love us now and always, to the end of all time.
Beat us down to nothing, take away these lives.
Love us now and forever, until the universe dies.
Take us then to heaven, and help us to see the light.

Delight In the Downfall

Press your lips against my heart.
Tear at my flesh and rip it apart.
Fuck my head now, just kill my dreams.
Open your mouth, to taste the insanity.

Delight in the downfall.
Of our beautiful world of music and rage.
Fuck all of this nonsense, which infests our dreams.
Open now to the answers, in which you wish not to see.

Press your lips against my heart.
Delight in the downfall, of everything that we are.
Fuck all of the torment, which keeps me from you.
Open your eyes to see now, that I'm deep inside of you...

Null the Pleasures

Plug into me and speak those words of pleasures and pains.
Let sanity die and watch as everything remains the same.
Tell me that I am something more to you than a freak.
Disconnect yourself from me to know, that we have now only pain.

With all pleasures fleeting, burning away just like our dreams.
Grace forgotten and bleeding, left wandering below the sea.
Tell me now that this all will mean something more in the end.
Tell me right now, that there was a reason as to why you left...

Plug into me and see that which I have seen for all of these years.
Listen to the riddle, and try your best to make your way through the fear.
I am not the hero, I am just a sad little waste of poetic laughter and cries.
Come with me and let us null all of the pleasures, *because we have died.*

Disconnect yourself from me, and then just cast me away.
Sing along with all of the lyrics, and they sound so insane.
For that is the epitome, of this poet's sick demented mind.
Come and null all the pleasures, then you can see through my eyes...

I Can Feel the Inside

Open your eyes to see this dying world.
Love me forever and yet only for now.
Reach beyond the torment for the pleasures of then.
Tell me that I mattered, and then just cast me away.

I can feel inside of this dying world.
It feels like pure insanity and rage.
I can see beyond this dying world.
And to tell you the truth, it's all the very same.

So open your eyes to see me standing here.
I am holding out my hand and still waiting for you to take it.
Reach out to me my love, if you can.
So together we can feel the birth of our world's beautiful ending.

Wrath & Other Pastimes

Spoken for those feeble minds, left in pain and out of time.
As all to be, of that dire thought left howling at the wake.
Come place your tongue into my mouth, and then what have we to say?
Of that bitter moment, that has dug its way out of the grave.

For to speak out against the norm, "It is now our time!"
Then to feel the constant burn, draining down this twisted spine.
It causes such a shock, to watch as our world melts away.
Then have now us only to laugh, over all our sick and lovely pains.

Was led to believe, *that there is something more waiting on the other side.*
Can hardly breathe, with smoke filling these lungs, so soon I might die.
So let us laugh, over all of this wrath and other sweet pastimes.
Come and place your tongue into my mouth, and what have we to say?

Of so many murders, gone on unseen by the minds that hope.
Upon this endless wrath, drowning now in the pools of smoke.
All is becoming so great, of a notion that can no longer make it.
So we just laugh upon the wrath and other great pastimes.

As the Moment Goes

As the moment passes on by like so many before it.
Our souls they die, but can we afford this?!
All hope is dead, just like all of our waking dreams.
As the moments pass on by, what left have we?!

As the moment goes, we wonder if we were ever real.
As the emotions fade, we just wish to awake.
As the notions gather, we just wanted to see the stars.
As the moment goes on by, we have now only these scars.

As the moment passes us by, we just want to open our eyes.
To see the beginning of the end of that which could never be.
As the moment goes on by, we just want to set ourselves free.
Free from pain and the fact that this world was never truly real...

166

Electronic Bleeding

Distorted whispers upon the razor as it is slitting.
Abnormal laughter echoes on, through the night it is sifting.
Hidden eyes watching on, as darkness consumes our dreaming.
Then as we open our wrist, we weep upon the electronic bleeding.

As horror has become, the only truth left in our lives.
We are dead and nothing else, so just turn off the lights.
Here in the nonsense, of our toxic head-trips constantly pushing.
We all sit back and enjoy the ride, into the electronic weeping.

Are we there yet, at that place that we call heaven?
Are we dead yet, or still waiting for that moment?
Is there any chance now, of telling my love that I am sorry?
Is there any chance, for me to tell you that I wish not to be forgiven?

With distorted whispers lingering on the tip of the razor as it is slitting.
Strange voices echo on, through the night they are forever sifting.
Upon the hidden meanings, as to why darkness has consumed our dreaming.
Then as we open our wrist, on goes the endless distorted screaming.
For we cannot stop, all the beautiful electronic bleeding...

Eulogizing

Standing at the feet of a God.
Questioning if I am truly worthy enough.
To feel its awesome touch upon my face.
Then I am so grateful to know this life was not a waste.

While I am singing this melody inside my head.
I begin to question if I was always dead.
As I am standing here at the feet of a God.
I truly begin to realize that I was always lost.

"Looking up and praying for guidance..."

Smiles All Bogus

She looked into my eyes, beyond all the pain.
She reached into my life, to take the hurt away.
She wanted me to stand, and be the better man.
She wanted me to smile, and never to look back.

I tried my best but failed, at everything in life.
I tried to stand but fell, and then I landed on that knife.
I tried to cry but couldn't, because nothing inside was left.
I tried to smile but couldn't, because it was all so bogus in the end.

She looked into my eyes, so far beyond all the pain.
She reached deep into my life, to take the pain away.
She wanted me to stand up, and to be the better man.
She wanted me to smile, and never to look back...

Breaking My Teeth Out

Breaking my teeth out, "I think I'm gonna die!?"
Pulling on that thread, only to watch myself unwind.
Telling myself that I'm okay, although I know it's a lie.
Breaking out my teeth, "Yes I think I'm gonna die!!"

Trying to keep myself in check, "I'm fucking freaking out!!!"
Trying to take in a deep breath, then the smoke I let out.
I can feel my flesh moving, something has got a hold of me.
I can feel as if I am decaying, as I'm breaking out all of my teeth...

The demons they are weeping, because I have them down.
The Devil he just wonders, when I will let him out.
As God does still want me, to let go and ask for forgiveness.
There is no changing what has happened and, "*I think I'm gonna die!!!*"

168

It Feels Like Horror

It feels like horror, dripping upon my lips.
It tastes like death, and with the acid it is mixed.
Watch as together we are burned, then forgotten again.
It seems as though, we are never to know what it is to be free.

Can you see the Armageddon, it is carved into my face.
Can you feel all of the horror, here within my grave?
Come and take us to that reason, of the silence felt today.
Come and let us end this, as we all just walk away.

It feels like horror, groping around inside my head.
It tastes like acid, all of the burning upon my breath.
Watch as we are fused together, and become one waste of life.
It seems as though all of this has already happened, once upon a time.

Can you see the end is coming, and I'm sure it has already gone?
Can you feel as we are burning, here in hell together and alone?
Come and take us to that moment, when we realize the truth.
Come and feel with us the horror, *which remains between me and you...*

Nuked

And with the wind our ashes are blown away.
Into tomorrow and far beyond all of this pain.
There is nothing that remains of us other than ash.
We are never to be remembered, only forgotten with the past.

We only lived for pleasure, and it did get us far indeed.
We all lived for freedom, but freedom was never free...
We had tried our best to stop it, the ending of our world.
We did fail ourselves, as now nothing remains anymore.

And with the wind our ashes are all blown away.
Into the never and far beyond our empty graves.
We didn't mean to, pull the switch and end our world.
We only wanted to be free, so now we are all at peace.
"Forevermore..."

Chapter 10

Sanity Mired

Torn Leaves

These *Eyes* slit wide open, now bleeding out all I've ever seen.
I am that demonic monster, hidden within all your troubled dreams.
We are waking at the ending, of our once pure world of peace.
Now there is nothing left for us, just another random torn leaf.

So can you feel it, as my whole world is dying under my flesh?
Can you see it, *the razor that has sunk below and remains still in my wrist?*
Tell me – can you taste it, the burn in the back of my throat?
Can you remember me? "I am that sad forgotten ghost."

These Eyes slit wide open, still bleeding out all I have seen.
I am that demonic creature, waiting in your every dream.
We are the ending, of everything that we have ever loved.
We are all but torn leafs, just wishing that we could burn...

So can you see it, the decay of all hope as I open my flesh?
Can you stop it, the endless bleeding from these wrists?
Tell me that I mattered, right before I forever fade away.
Can you remember me? "I am the ghost that never had a face..."

"I am you – my love, just another torn leaf..."

Said With Hate

When you told me "I love you" it was said with hate.
When death had come, I knew that we were too late.
When I held you close, that is when I truly felt alive.
When you had walked away, I felt only my heart begin to die.

When I was a dreamer, you told me to just keep on fighting.
When I made it all come true, that is when *our love* started dying.
When I was the weak one, you told me to stand and to be strong.
When I kissed you, that is when I knew that we had gone too far.

When you told me "I love you" it was said with hate.
When I tried my best to let go, that is when I learned of our fate.
When you wanted me to be there, I was there to hold you close.
When you told me that you "love me", *it was said with hate so very cold...*

Our Time Is Over

Our time is over, gone and passed.
Our lives were jokes, so let us laugh.
Our love is pointless, as now it fades.
Our hearts are dead now, so turn the page.

We've come miles, to reach this point in time.
We've said so many things, but how many of them were lies?
We've only wanted, to be there when the credits roll.
We've come to an ending, and now it's growing cold.

Our time has come, gone and passed away.
Our eyes are blind now, and we can't hear what they say.
Our love it was pointless, because it was all just a lie.
Our time is over, so just turn the page...

Can't Name the Feeling

I can't describe this feeling, groping around inside my head.
I can't feel my fingers, they are numb, "so maybe I am dead."
I can't be the scapegoat forever, because I soon will no longer exist.
I can't be the one to save you, because I can't even save myself...

You are the only reason, that I am still in this damned world.
You are my only reason, as to why I wander around in this void.
You are the angel, which is stabbing me endless in my heart.
You are the true reason, as to why I was torn apart.

I can't name this feeling, *which has me beating my head against the floor.*
I can't hear what you are saying, *as you are standing behind that open door.*
I can't describe this torment, *in which I have lived with all my life.*
I can't be the one to save you, *if I can't even find a way to save myself.*

174

So I Try to Remember

So I try to remember, as I place the LSD under my skin.
I try to forget you, so we can fall in love all over again.
You are so beautiful, I can't even begin to illustrate it.
You are my whole world, and with the acid you are washed away.

So I try to remember, all of what it was that happened in our past.
I try to let go, of all the pain that has been building within.
You are so gorgeous, I can't even begin to describe it.
You are the death of me my love, and I would never change it.

As I try to remember, what it was like to be in true love and grace.
I can only remember, all the acid that had taken my soul away.
As you were laughing, I lied there weeping – broken alone the floor.
You did never exist my love, *you were only a beautiful forgotten dream...*
"Still - I try to remember."

In The Black-Lights

Come with me and call to the little...
Mushroom creatures that roam the fields behind my home.
Come and reach with me into the...
Middle of the past that we had burned and left so very cold.
Come to the end now and scream...
As all the pretty colors shine so significantly upon the walls.
Come and drink of the black-lights....
And now you can see the death of our fragile little souls.
Come with me and let us go there...
To that place where only demons and angels understand the rights.
Come and take us to that darkness...
As we trip onwards upon all the beautiful black-lights.
Come now and follow all the little mushroom creatures deep into my head...

Conversing With Death

Communicating in voice that I don't understand.
I am just a fucking bastard, spewing out another rant.
I am speaking with death, and he said it was about your time.
Conversing with all the voices, here in my twisted mind.

I have seen the end of the tunnel, and there was no light.
I have kissed the lips of angels, but then they all died.
I have reached into the nonsense, which is infesting my dead dreams.
I have spoken with death, and it all sounded like beautiful insanity...

Communicating with the shadows, dancing about inside my head.
Speaking with the voices, which are telling me, that I am dead.
I can only laugh now, *because I have seen what is waiting for us at the end.*
I have conversed with death, and this is what he had to say...

Obtain New Verdicts

I was there, I know what they did.
I was there, and the crime they did commit.
I watched as they had murdered.
But there was nothing I could do to stop it.
I was there to watch it all, and I know what they did.

We must obtain new verdicts, right here and now.
We must set all the wrongs right, we must do this now.
There is no changing what was done on that day.
They had murdered an innocent, and they must pay.
We must obtain new verdicts, or they could walk free...

They will pay for their crimes.
"They will pay..."

Shoot Me Please!

Please shoot me in the wrist, to bleed me dead.
Take me back to hell, that beautiful place in my head.
I have tried to be your hero, but I failed to save the day.
So I guess I'm just a villain, and that will never change.

So shoot me in my heart, to watch me bleed dry.
Cut me into little pieces, then cover me with lime.
Take me back to that moment, when we became one.
So I can just laugh, and put a real bullet into that gun.

Please shoot me now, to end all of this fucked up pain.
Please take me back to hell, that wonderful place in my brain.
I did try to be your lover, but I wasn't what you had wanted.
I did become your enemy, and then you walked away...

So please shoot me now, to end this fucking torment!
Take me deeper into hell, where I know that I am welcome.
I have tried to be a hero, but I couldn't save you on that day.
So I guess I'll be your villain, and that will never change...

Down to Nothing

I am worthless, now down to nothing.
I am a pointless, chance to see a new day.
I was an angel, now but only a sad demon.
I am only, the true end to this pointless story.

We had seen the outcome, but it didn't get us anywhere.
We had felt the touch of the heavens, but then it all ended.
We had wanted to be together, forever and for always.
We had then realized, that we are now down to nothing.

I am worthless, now only a pathetic little bore.
I am a pointless, chance of seeing maybe something more.
I was a dreamer, whom did never get a chance to sleep.
So now I am a sleeper, down to nothing but more dead dreams...

With the Reasons

Was left there, broken at the end of the hall.
Was weeping so cold, covered in frost.
Was nothing more, than a bitter waste of time.
Was forgotten with the reasons, of why we are even here...

In shame was left screaming, to the great moon above.
In evil I am bathing, covered in the angel's blood.
Like the Devil I am waiting, for us all to just come undone.
Then there will be nothing left but sorrow and pain...

Like that time, when you had slapped my face.
Like that time when you told me to just fade away.
Like that moment, when I was standing at the end of the hall so cold.
Like God had once told me, "I will die alone."

Was left there, broken and weeping in shame.
Was nothing more, than a shadow with a name.
Was there ever a time, when our love meant something more?
Was left there forgotten with the reasons, of why we are still here...

Stop the Madness

Let's stop the madness, right here and now.
Let's eat the human flesh, and we'll find out.
There is no honor, there is only the pleasure of rage.
Come and take my hand, and let's get the fuck away.

To the other side of our sanities, so very grim.
Into another tragedy, beneath our dirty skin.
There is now only the madness, here within my heart.
Come and let us go there, far beyond the stars.

Let's stop all of the wars now, because there is no point.
Let's enjoy all of this madness, because it won't end.
There is now only the pleasure, of eternal anger and rage.
Come take my hand now, and let us fly away...

Severing Connections

The notions sink in deep, now connections are severed.
The potions taste so sweet, as they bring me closer to the graveyard.
Our minds they are twisting, and soon enough they shall break.
We are no longer connected, to what they call faith.

God he wants me to be there, to watch as our world burns.
The Devil he is laughing, because we never did learn.
Our hearts are now forever screaming, for hope and to be saved.
But we are no longer connected, to what they call faith.

As on now with more bitter emotions, felt as the death of our souls.
We are all falling so much deeper, we can never again be whole.
Our minds are all poisoned, and there is no chance that it will be okay.
For we had spent our whole lives, severing our connections with faith...

She Preferred the Lie

She was most happy, when I was far away.
She wanted only my death, and for me to be fazed away.
She liked it better, when I was never there.
She wanted me to be but a ghost, a fragment of the past.

Our love was so misguided, nothing but a fake.
I was but only a fighter, realizing his bitter fate.
There was truly nothing, in which I could say to make it better.
She preferred the lie, because I was never worth it...

We had tried our best to be there, and love each other forever more.
I know the truth of what was hidden, there behind that door.
It is a fact, in which my heart still wishes to deny.
She never did truly love me, she only preferred the lie...

"So now what have I...?"

Devastation

Vast minds of the reason, only destruction and decay.
Tired points of frustration, as I lie awake in this grave.
Bring to me the ending, because I've had enough of this shit.
Constant acts of devastation, digging into my wrists.

Have I not been there, to the last levels of hell?
Have I not tasted the pleasures, of the whiskey and rusted nails?
I have walked for ages, upon this damned road of leaves.
I have spoken with the dead, and they told me it will be okay.

As into more of a dire, mindset that makes us feel only hate.
We speak now in tongues, and only the Devil knows what we say.
So bring me there, on-top that hill and beneath a tall tree.
So as I decay we shall become one, blissful and free.

With vast minds of pure darkness, they see now into our dead souls.
We are all just weary creatures, freezing alone so very cold.
I have been there, upon the truth and what lies ahead.
I have tasted the devastation, which still lingers upon your breath...

"We can never be forgiven."

Can We Save?

Can we save this world, before it comes to an end?
Can we save ourselves, from committing more sins?
Can we save our souls, or are we all damned to burn?
Can we save each other, or will we just never fucking learn?

Can we stop all of this, endless destroying of our hearts?
Can we love each other truly, or will we just tear each other apart?
Can we make any difference, or will it all in the end be the same?
Can we open our fucking eyes, so maybe we can see!?

"We must work together..."

Inundated

All I am is fucking wasted.
All I've had was fucking taken.
Still to this day I'm constant moving.
Pushing to find the answers you seek.
Someday we might arrive there.
Upon a new point of eternity.

All I am just fucking hated.
All I've done was left fucking bleeding.
So here I am now just constant screaming.
Pushing forward into more dreaming.
Still hoping that someday I might just find it.
The truth of the fact and we are alone...

So all I am is fucking wasted.
Still I'm screaming as I know I am hated.
So what the fuck now can I do to change this?
All I want is to be at peace again.
But still I have more to do before I'm finished.
And all I want now is to end this pain...

Return to Stratosphere

You bitches never learned shit about being high.
As I return to the stratosphere, I know I am gonna die.
And I realize now, just what it means to be free.
The true purpose of this life is much clearer to me.
"And all that is left is death and insanity..."
As tonight is the night, in the stratosphere we'll fight.
Truly all along we were nothing more than ghosts.
We are dead and we know now what it is to be free.

In the stratosphere we, fly!
Hold on baby, because I don't wanna die!
In the stratosphere we, fly!
Hold on baby, because I don't wanna die!
In the stratosphere we, fly!
Return now with me and feel the truth of being high.
In the stratosphere, we die...
"Good night."

Depository

Endless amounts of anger and pain.
But tell me where does it all go?
Lost thoughts of when we let go that day.
But tell me where have we gone?

Here at the bottom of this hellish pit.
I begin to notice that I'm not alone.
There are creatures that roam this land.
They are hungry and they want my flesh.

So take me please to another side of this pain.
Let me find what it means to truly be alive.
I know that I truly am the one to blame.
I am the truth hidden behind the lie.

As endless amounts of anger and pain still grow.
Tell me, in the end where does it all go?
Lost out there somewhere and maybe never to be found.
Where does it all go, and how do we get out?!

Perverted Ideals

I think there is a reason to the scars on your lips.
I think it's kind of cute, when you give it that kiss.
I think there is more to it, yet you will never tell.
I know my views are kind of perverted, but oh fucking well.

I think it is awesome, when you dance like that.
I do enjoy it, when you shake your hips.
I very much like it, when you look up at me.
I do indeed love it, when you're down on your knees.

I think there is a reason behind that look in your eyes.
I think you must enjoy how it tastes, and you know I am right.
I guess there is no more of a point now, only pleasure and pain.
I do believe though, you must enjoy how it tastes...

There Is No Salvation

There is no salvation, we are on our own.
There is no hope left, we cannot save our souls.
We are damned and forgotten, by even God himself.
There is no salvation, no escaping this tormented hell.

We have been forsaken, time and time again.
We have been left astray, damned for all our sins.
We cannot save us, so there is no point to even try.
We know it is hopeless, but still we stand and fight.

There is no salvation, because we've destroyed all chance.
There is no hope left, so on and on we just rant.
We are lost and forgotten, by even our very selves.
There is no salvation, here in the depths of hell.

We have done this, maybe all by mistake.
We have awakened, but we were just too late.
We cannot change this, the sad facts of our dismay.
We know it is all pointless, but we fight on anyway...

Crimson Teardrops

Seek the honor, where ever it may be.
Speak to the nonsense, which makes me you and you, me.
Take of that moment, learn something if you can.
Return to the beginning, of this war once again.

Touch of that creature, she loves how it feels.
Fuck all of the meanings, because these wounds cannot heal.
So be one with your hatred, and love every second that does pass.
Weep the crimsons tears with me my love.
And then we both shall laugh...

"Laugh."

Left At the Wake

I am weeping, left at the wake.
I just want to remember, her beautiful face.
She was my whole world, now I'm stuck in space.
I am truly alone out here, and that is my fate.

For I am the bastard, that laughed as our world came to an end.
I am the monster, which feasted upon all our sins.
I am the nonsense, that pushed its way into the light.
I truly am the reason, that all of our love had died.

So here I wait weeping, alone at the wake.
There I go screaming, because I can't stop the pain.
She was my *everything*, my whole fucking world.
I am truly alone now, because I threw her away.

So I am nothing more, than a sick sideshow freak.
I am the fact, of why it is that our souls still bleed.
I am indeed, the nonsense that began to make sense.
I am left alone at the wake, and "*that's what I get...*"

Creatures Of the Past

Endless nightmares of the creatures of my past.
I think they're returning, I feel they are coming back.
All the little creatures, which haunt me still to this day.
They are returning, to come and take me away.

As endless goes all the fearing, the creatures of my past.
They are back now, and hiding myself won't last.
They know where to find me, they are coming and I can't stop them.
They are here now, and there is nothing I can do at all.

All the creatures of my past, still they wander around inside my head.
They are angry, and they want now to take control.
I cannot stop them any longer, too far passed the point of no return.
I think I'm gonna freak out, as I feel them eating my soul.
"*They're back...*"

184

Her Lips Said-Not

Gazing into my eyes, beyond the fear.
Lost within myself, for so many years.
As weeping out the pain, so many frozen tears.
Gazing beyond the last hour, and now I see it clear.

There is no chance of saving, a love that did never exist.
There is no point in wanting, time to end this test.
We cannot stop the bleeding, it's gushing out by the gallon.
We have no hope left, so I guess we are truly fucked.

Her lips said-not, then our whole world began to rot.
Our flesh it did burn, because we never did learn.
How to be truly at peace, as for these pains we can never ease.
So I guess in the end, there was in deed no point at all.

So laugh all the way, deeper into our graves.
We've fallen into the pit, beyond this life of shit.
There was never any chance, only these pointless rants.
So now we know, that sanity was a pointless dream.

Sexual Punishments

Said as more than the emotions called pain.
Feelings echoing on, far passed the grave.
It is a notion, in which so many have died for.
It is a pleasure, which most will never experience.

Then it goes on tearing, at the back of this mind.
Then we go on screaming, following the rhyme.
We are connected, and it feels just right.
Yet this is a punishment, for all of our crimes.

It is said to be a pain, in which most would kill for.
It is a great sustain, moving on and on through the night.
We are forever in pleasure, knowing that we deserve this.
It is a punishment, in which we impose upon ourselves...

On Vanity

Narcissistic as I always have been.
Standing on top of the world, with all beneath my feet again.
I am the greatest, thing that will ever ensue in your life.
I am that moving voice, echoing behind your eyes.

On vanity you are calling, to the pit for an answer.
In rage you are thrashing, with pride growing like a cancer.
In vain you are pushing, your twisted ideals upon the world.
On goes the nonsense, swimming about within this void.

For I am the only, thing that can make a difference at this point.
I am the one you need to listen to, I am your inner voice.
You must listen to me, or you are damned to fail.
I am your God and your Devil, I am both your heaven and your hell...

With Whom

With whom am I speaking with at this time?
With your rusted needles, you are poisoning my spine.
But now I am numbed, just laughing and weeping.
Now all wars will soon be done, because everything is burning away.

With whom have I been speaking, "you" the one behind the page?
With whom am I weeping, here so cold and in pain?
Was there ever a chance to end the cutting, here within this mind?
With whom am I screaming, "That we have reached our time..."

We are all together worthless, just a fucking waste of life.
We were all together burning, and now far passed the line.
So with whom am I speaking, here inside my own twisted head?
With whom am I laughing? Because the both of us are dead...

" Who are you..?"

Until It Goes Away...

Forever stay, within this hell driven mind.
Forever fall, between reality and the lie.
Forever love, the demon with angel wings.
Forever know, that there is more than what we see.

This mind twists and turns within my soul.
Full of hate and insanity.
Until it goes away, "I will forever stay..."

Twist and turn of my psyche, as I forever hold you down.
You hate me only because I'm "Me"...
A sad freak with my mind twisting and fucking turning.
So forever I shall stay, to be a thorn in your side...

This mind twists and turns within my soul.
Full of hate and insanity.
Until it goes away, "I will forever stay..."

1900 Spiders

I can't even go one fucking day now.
Without breaking down into tears.
It's been so very long, tens of painful years.
My life it seems a bit grimmer.
Still I wait here alone, wallowing around in all my sins...

"So it's a throw-back," just another way to end this act.
With chapters falling from these eyes like the tears I weep.
Again I go, filling another sheet with blood and ink.
1900 spiders, crawling around within my veins.

Break me, then let my number be called!
Hate me, and then laugh as we both fall!
Rape my, heart and then let it break!
Take my, soul and I hope we're not too late...!

I have gone too far, and truly these demons know the way.
A million voices in my head, 1900 spiders within my mind...

Chapter 11

10-90

Something's Under the House

There is something, under the house.
Something kicking and screaming under the house.
I can't quite make out what it is, but I know that it wants to get out.
The strange thing that is thrashing around, under the house.

It just wants to get out, *thrashing about as if something is trying to kill it.*
It just wants to get out, because it's so dark where it is right now.
I can hear it moaning, trying to find its way out.
I can hear it, the strange thing that is under the house.

Something seems so familiar, about the way it is screaming.
Something is telling me that I've been here, it's so odd indeed.
I can't take this, the constant clatter and weeping from under the house.
But now it is quiet, because it must be dead...

Carcass In the Street

Voices echo, of that deep hurt reaming from our past.
So many, times of venturing out there where nothing is left.
It's much, further away than we'd want to admit to.
And to this day, it still remains out there where no one can see it.

Of that moment, we had watched our world become so faint.
Of that torment, that still remains within my brain.
We cannot deny it, all of the pain that we still hold to this day.
We cannot change it, the grim fact that the pain will never fade.

There is a carcass out there, lying in the middle of a street.
It's been there for so long, cooking away in the hot sun.
There is a torment we still keep, and a truth that we can't deny.
There is a pain that we cannot end, *so we hold it forever through our lives.*

"Our brother shall be avenged."

Add Blue...

Un-questions forgetting the reasons behind the lines.
The world became cold and we had all gone blind.
Frozen in hell over the fact of a tragic means to an ends.
We have all gone blind and we can never see again.

Lost wandering and we just don't know to where.
We have all been forgotten yet we know no one else is out there.
We are damned and shall remain as such forevermore.
We are all so very cold and alone down here, weeping on the floor.

Can ever this mind remember something other than pain?
Maybe I should let go and just fall to my fate.
Can please this mind remember a time of great love and peace.
In this mind remains only a vision of blue and that too now fades.

As all to be left screaming alone here in pain.
We have all wandered so far out that we may never make it back.
It is so very cold down here, with the blade still inside my wrist.
So then add some blue, and remember that *we might* be missed...

Not Far From Hope

Not far from hope, just a few more steps away.
Not far from the ending, just maybe a few more days.
Not a chance for peace, that was but only a dream.
Not ever can we change this, the ending yet to be.

Not far from hope, we almost can reach it.
Not a day has gone by, when we haven't fought for it.
Not a time now, for us to wait around for nothing.
Not ever again, will "*that time*" we regain.

We're not far now from hope.
Not far now from hope.
Far from hope...

Fucking Swine

Back to that torment of the needles in my spine.
Back to the death of our world and the end of all time.
Back to the death of logic and the fuel to our dismay.
Back to our deaths we go, six feet within our graves.

Fuck all this bullshit, it doesn't make any sense.
Fuck all of your pity and all the lies upon your breath.
Fuck all of humanity, just pointless fucking swine.
Fuck all of everything, and bring now the end of times...

Back to that torment of the needles in my spine.
Back to that moment when we had crossed the line.
Back to our deaths now, six feet below in our graves.
Back to our beginnings, so maybe our ending we can save.

Spirits Remain

Left in pain, still spirits remain.
Over the edge, inside this head.
All demons they howl, within me so loud.
I do not believe that I can ever be the same again.

In pain is this heart, so very torn apart.
In death was the lie, truth hidden in life.
All hope now is gone, so just sing along.
Because in the end both our fates shall be the same.

Still in sorrow, as all the spirits remain.
Lingering on, upon the tip of my tongue.
The burn is so sweet, and it still haunts all my dreams.
The truth that remains beneath the frozen lake...

"You need but only to remember."

Uninvited Memories

Visions dissolving within my head, it causes me so much pain and dread.
As I am flooded with memories that I have been trying so hard to forget.
It hurts me so fucking bad that I very much believe I am going to be sick.
God help me to destroy all of these uninvited memories inside my head.

Can we all together take that blade and cut these memories out from my mind?
Is there anyone still out there, somebody that I can believe is standing on my side?
I feel so very alone here inside of myself screaming into the void and no one hears.
So I step over that ledge and I just have to smile because I know you don't care.

Endless visions swarming around inside my head, causing so much pain and dread.
And again I wake here alone in my bed, lost and screaming in someone else's head.
Where have I been going, the story has changed and I need to get out again.
Help me now to kill all of these uninvited memories which now haunt my death.

Visions dissolving within my head and still you try to tell me it's just a dream.
On goes all of the screaming, as for so very long I have been here still bleeding.
And still I just want it to be true, that I have indeed only been dreaming.
Get me out of myself, just pull the trigger so we can end the uninvited memories.

Twisted TimeLine

Let's speak of those pains and fears of our troubled pasts.
Let's take another pill and just pray that it might last.
We are falling into hell again and there is no saving us this time.
So I guess we need only to smile as we go tripping over the line.

Let's speak to the Devil and tell him that he was but a waste of time.
Let's hold onto each other and remember all of our pointless cries.
It's been so long now that we can't even recall where it all started.
Damn these twisted timelines, takes us only back to pain and rage.

Let's speak with God now and forever we shall await his reply.
Let's just say that the story is over and that we had a great time.
We are forever falling into our minds and away from any hope.
So I guess we need only to smile as we remember what we truly are...

194

Odd Noises

Listen close to the odd noises inside my head.
Can you hear them as they dance upon my breath?
Listen close to the odd noises that still remain within.
Can you save me *my love*, or am I truly alone once again?

Grasp of that notion, it's digging its way out.
Take of that motive, then we are let down.
Kill all of the nonsense, here blistering inside my heart.
Listen to the odd noises, which have been with me from the start.

Hold on tight to your love again, it's soon going to burn away.
Can we not just say we are sorry, and then step away?
Take note of all the odd noises, still echoing within my brain.
Can you save me this time *my love*, or am I fucked once again?

"Such odd – odd noises..."

With the Snow It Melted

Darkness upon this night, so early in the morning.
Loneliness in this life, that is nothing new to me.
The rage it takes control, from time to time.
It is dark out tonight, dark and so very cold.

So what to do with these bitter emotions.
It has been so long now and still those memories haunt me.
And with the snow all love for her had melted away.
So tell me why, why am I still here screaming in pain!?

Left to be so sick, dreaming upon another moon-trip.
And with the snow all of my emotions had melted away.
So now I am numb, so cold and numb in my open grave.
As to this day, the memories of her beautiful face still haunt me.

"Someday We'll Make It."

Someday we'll make it, and we will hold the world in our hands.
Someday we'll wake up, and realize that this was all but a dream.
Someday we'll reach it, the true ending of this damn relentless war.
Someday we'll make it, and we will together rule this world.

Someday had "*come & gone*" and nothing is left but me.
Time it is truly cruel, now what could be left to say?
There was no honor, only the fact of that twisted moment.
Dreaming that we will someday make it and rule this world.

On more of those harsh actions, we have only the end of pain.
Then birth of a new emotion, something that hurts far passed the grave.
We are all together at fault I say, we are damned souls indeed.
Damned for the killing of our dreams, "*by making them into realities.*"

Someday we'll make it, and we won't have to worry anymore.
Someday we'll make it, and see what was behind that open door.
Someday we'll wake up, and realize that this was all but a dream.
Someday has "*come & gone,*" and nothing is left now but me...

"Nothing..."

Under A Bridge

Skeletons in my closet and under my bed.
A door cracked open inside of my troubled head.
My eyes are left wide-shut to see through the *truth.*
The lie you choose to bite into is now far too sweet for your tooth.
With sympathy held sweet to only those whom knew.
A skeleton under a bridge, "*between me and you...*"

So unfold the paper and sing that old tune.
Bring back to me those memories and beat my soul through.
Off to that road covered in those *dead dry-leaves.*
The one I had helped you to build beyond all those dreams.
And "Goodbye" didn't quite make it, "*but I'll see you again someday.*"
Though I know that I couldn't, still I had tried to escape.
Now locked *under the bridge* of *that song.*
So I guess I'm here to stay, just so you can hear me say.
"*Goodbye my friend, I'll see you again someday...*"

Intelligent Nonsense

For things to be that dire, have we not the will to take it?
Into another hour, of lying on the floor and screaming!
Screaming into my own mind, telling me to just let it go.
For not of any other reasons, I shall remain here frozen and alone.

With these knives I've been dreaming, of finding release on that day.
With the pain I've been dying, dying alone and it's all the same.
In death shall be found the answer, to the questions *that make up my soul.*
Then in an instant, the lights go out and can never be turned on again...

So fucking worthless, all of the attempts at saving our dead-love.
Still I just want to be rid of the memories, of what had been done.
All I truly ask for, is some intelligence to this endless nonsense.
I need to just let it all go, and then admit that I am dead...

For things to be that truly dire, have we not the will to take it?
Into another pointless hour, of lying on the floor, just screaming!
Screaming into my own mind, telling me that I need to just let it go.
And it is for that reason, that I shall remain here frozen and alone.

Forever alone...

As They Left

As they all walked away, I knew my life was over.
As they all walked away, I felt my inner-self begin to die.
As they left me, I could only move forward through the pain.
As they left me in the darkness, I realized that I was truly alone.

As they walked away, I knew that my life was over.
As they walked away, I knew that my heart was indeed dead.
As they left me to die alone, I decided to move onward instead.
As they left me, I knew that at that point my new life would begin.

As onward I move through the darkness and endless pain.
I move onward to be alive once again.
And they just left me...

197

Been Here For Ages

We've been here for ages, watching as our world dies.
We've been here for ages, and maybe it was a waste of our time.
We've been falling for ages, still wishing that we could reach an end.
We've been damned for ages, because of all our pointless sins.

I have seen beyond the nightmare, and I know now the truth.
I have reached into the darkness, and that is where I found you.
I am a dead poet, remembering what it was to be alive.
I have been beyond the ending, in fear, sorrow and no lights.

Been here for ages, watching our world just burn and die.
Been here for ages, telling her how much I love her smiles.
Been here for ages, watching as my life is being taken away.
Been here for ages, so now it's time for me to leave this place.

Inane Sacrifices

All my sacrifices haunting me endlessly in my head.
I've tried my hardest and I can't get any sleep at night.
Maybe it's because of the voices that go on screaming in me.
Or maybe it's the fact that this all might be a dream.

I want to wake up, and not feel so beaten and used.
I want to wake up, and be done with all memories of you.
I want to just get out, and stop feeling so cold and dead.
I want to get up, and leave all memories of you in the past.

All of my pointless sacrifices still haunt me late at night.
I can't get any sleep, so I just scream endlessly into the night.
That I am fighting, fighting so hard to keep myself together.
I need to escape this, before my head fucking explodes!

I want to wake up, and leave all of this pain behind.
I want to wake up, and be not so gone and wasted.
I want to just get out, to feel something more than this.
I want to forget you, my love I had sacrificed so you could be free.
I want to be forgotten, and to no longer exist in this insanity...

Walking the Loop

Gotta get away for a while, need some quiet time.
Gotta get away from here, to somewhere nice and secluded.
I need to leave all of the pain and screaming, I need to get out.
I need to leave behind all of this bullshit and pointless negative drives.

So I'm just walking the loop now, to get away for awhile.
Walking the loop, so I can end all of the pointless bitching.
Walking the loop now, knowing that I'll just end up _back where I started._
Still I'm walking to loop, just to get away for awhile.

Gotta get my head on right, there's too much at stake.
Gotta get my life together, so my death will mean something someday.
Gotta end all of the hurting, because the past is now passed.
Gotta just get it all out, so I can be at peace once again.

So I'm walking the loop, remembering all the times of our laughter.
Walking the loop, knowing that I'm getting so much closer.
Walking the loop, back to where all of this torment began.
I'm walking to loop now, hoping it will bring me back to you...

Useless Control

Watching such a great freak-out!
Then our words hold no more sense.
"What a great breakdown."
You - thinking that you're the only one that can be right.
Such a useless notion you're pushing.
But we aren't going to take that shit.
You need to just shut up!
Because you're not the only one in this world.
You need to fucking listen!
Listen to all of the people around you.
Because you are such a fucking head-trip!
Pushing your useless control onto us.
But we're not going to take this shit anymore...

Coke-Straw

A little straw up my nose, digging into my brain.
Then the beautiful powder, erases all of the pain.
So now I'm tripping, feeling like they're out to get me.
I think I'm gone now, far beyond pleasure and into insanity.

My body is shaking, lying on the floor in the middle of the room.
My heart it is racing, every time I begin to think *of "You."*
My soul it was taken, before I even knew that it did exist.
My world it is breaking, crumbling into nothing before my very eyes.

A little straw up my nose, scrambling up my brains.
Then it mixes with the coke, and it drives me so fucking insane!
So yes I'm very much tripping, I'm fucking freaking out!
I think that I am dead now, I am dead and soon I'm going to awake...

With hatred driving, all notions of love into the dirt.
In my heart left to wither, all of my memories of *"Her."*
So I do believe that my world is ending, right here and now.
So I just breathe it all in, then in my own blood I drown.

"I am dead with a smile on my face."

"I Would Have Died!"

I would have died if I didn't leave that very moment.
I would have died if I had opened my eyes to see what stood before me.
I would have told her truly how I feel if I had the chance again.
I would have died if I didn't drop what I was doing *and leave that moment.*

I would have died if I didn't leave you the way I did.
It killed me indeed to have to tell you that it was over.
I would have loved you until the very end of time.
I would have died if I had stayed and lived a lie.

"I would have died. I would have died..."

It Started Here

Tens of years ago it all started here.
So very much has changed over time.
But somehow I know that I'm still the same person.
The person that wanted to hold you close until the end of time.

Tens of years ago it all started here.
In this emotion I've been for so very many long years.
It had all started here in this twisted stated of mind.
But I know I'm still the same person that had died for *our love*.

Tens of years ago I had made a promise.
A promise in which I very much intend to keep.
It all started here with me standing so very tall with pride.
Now we're back where it all started and nothing much has changed.

Tens of years ago I had loved you to death and then I died.
It all started here in this twistedly brilliant state of mind.
In this emotion I've been for so long and it feels all the same.
It all started here where I told you "*I love you.*"
"*And from that day on, nothing could ever remain the same…*"

Why Can't You Hear Me?

Tell me truly, in the end what am I?
As I scream to you, tell me why can't you hear me!?
I've been trying so hard for you to just see me.
But I go on screaming and screaming!
So tell me now, why can't you hear me!?
I fucking love you, is that not enough?!
Why can't you hear me, *I'm still screaming, still weeping, still bleeding.*
And no matter what I say or do, it's all just pointless.
Because you must not care at all what it is that I've been fighting for?!
Why can't you understand me, it's really not that fucking hard!?
Why can't you hear me, I'm standing right here in front of your face.

Maybe it's true, that I really am dead.
Dead to you my love, I'm dead to you…

Holly Burning

Years of cutting, I hope that I'm learning.
Years of fighting, but no one else is here but me.
Years of knowing, the facts of our inevitable ends.
Years of laughing, because it's all just so damn funny to me.

Then we all go tripping, into the smoke we venture.
We all go tripping, far away and beyond the unknown.
We are all gone and wasted, laughing at the clouds of smoke.
We are laughing so demonic, because we are gone and never to return.

It's like "*that time*" when we had spoke, spoken with God himself.
He told us to let go, to let go and fall away and to laugh.
To laugh at our torments, because we're doing it all to ourselves.
We're doing it all to ourselves, killing our dreams and burning them away.

These years of cutting, cutting deep into my heart.
I hope that I've been learning, "*if not,*" then what was the point?
I love the fact, the fact that all I've ever loved is now burning.
Everything is burning, our whole world - our past and futures.
Everything is burning... Just burning away...

Haunted People

I cannot escape all of the demons of my past.
I cannot take this forever, I want my life back!
I need to end all of these unbearable torments.
God get me out of my head for one fucking day!

Like a sweet little whisper it happens upon my heart.
Like a kiss that will be forever cherished, it leaves me so scared.
For there is no changing the nature of a negative emotion.
There is no saving me, because I know that I deserve this.

I cannot escape all of the demons of my past.
I cannot change it, the words upon my last breath.
I need to escape this, all of the torments I endure.
I need escape myself, so my heart can rest in peace.

202

Retracing My First Steps

All this time and where did it get me?
All of those lies, they still fucking eat at me.
Ain't that a bitch, that there is no changing the past.
On we are still moving, and that is that.

Retracing my first steps, to see if I had forgotten something.
Something left behind in our past, a way for me to reach you.
I'm retracing my first steps, to find a fragment of my forgotten youth.
A youth that was spent fighting to just survive this war...

All of this time and where the fuck did it get me!?
All of your lies, they are still fucking eating me.
I'm trying to go back, and see if there is something that I missed.
Something that can bring me closer to you my love.

Retracing my first steps to learn a little more about myself.
Retracing my first steps so that I can know truly who I am.
I'm trying to go back again, and save our damned past.
I want to say that I can save us my love, but that is just a dream...

Brothers Fighting

Brothers fighting, that's nothing at all new.
Brothers fighting, over the same shit that we always do.
Brothers growing, away over time.
Brother still fighting, even if there is no reason to fight.

Brothers trying, to be there for each other.
Brothers knowing, that soon we will all part ways.
Brothers laughing, at all of our fun little games.
Brothers always fighting, fighting together for always.

Brothers fighting, over who is the strongest.
Brothers fighting, so that the others don't feel the pain.
Brothers laughing, laughing all our fears away.
Brothers leaving, we are all now leaving.
"And brother, I will see you again someday..."

"Save Our Sanities!"

What happened to the voice that told me that I was real?
What happened to that love of mine, *"she is waiting for me on-top a hill..."*
What ever happened to just loving each other to the very end of time?
God save our sanities, before we're all out of time.

What happened to that notion, of holding pride true in my heart?
What has become of me my love, I feel so fucking torn apart.
What has become of you, so very lost and mentally distorted.
God get me out of this nightmare, *before I realize I've always been awake.*

What has happened to just letting it all go and then walking away.
What has happened to the voice in my heart, it must have gone away.
What now has become of me, I feel so sick and distorted.
God save my sanity or I shall be nothing more.

What has happened to this world in which I once loved so dear?
What has become of you my love, *"are you still out there waiting on me?"*
What ever happened to just saying I love you, and then all is fine.
God just kill my sanity, and then take away my life...

Drunk & Insignificant

That's it, that right there.
That's the way I want to remember you.
You - looking down at me laughing.
Laughing at me because I am drunk and insignificant.
I am drunk because I am lost and have nowhere to go.
No place that I can call my own, I am abandoned.

That's it, that's the way I want to remember you.
You – laughing at me because I am drunk and insignificant.
That's it, that's the way I will always remember us.
Fucking broken, a worthless notion in which was thrown away.
I am drunk and insignificant, nothing but a waste.
A waste of both of our time...

"That's the way I want to remember us."

Falling Into the Gutter

Stumbling across town, for no apparent reason.
That missing piece never found, but I know that it's out there.
Our words were never clear, but we said them anyway.
Our world has burned, and we are but only ashes in our graves.

Falling into the gutter, that is where you'll find me.
Falling into the gutter, that is where she put me.
There by myself with no one, only my fears and pains.
So what then of our love I say, it too must have burned away.

Stumbling across town, trying to find that missing piece.
Drunk and abandoned, cold upon this unending night.
I'm falling into the gutter, so that is where you can find me.
Falling into the gutter, because that is where she put me.

"Six Miles From Home."

"On the way passed the graveyard."
Odd now to say that it shall always be remembered.
"On the way passed the graveyard."
Strange to say that it has been so long of a time.

Six miles from home, then the whole story changed.
Six miles from home, then in a very instant...
The lights went out, and our world became cold.
Six miles from home, then a sudden twist ending...

"On the way passed the graveyard."
For some reason fate had stepped in and changed our lives forever.
"On the way passed the graveyard."
For some reason that chapter of time had then ended.
And God took him away...

" Our fallen brother lives on forever in us."

Chapter 12

Within a Decade

Judge My Actions

Judge my actions then cast me away.
Reach into my tattered past, now can you feel my pains?
Love me true for I am but a child.
A child that has seen far beyond the gates of hell.

Take my last words then engrave them into my headstone.
Laugh at me while I burn, because I'm just so fucking worthless.
Can now our paths collide once again, because *I truly do miss you.*
Can now I just let it all go and then admit that you were only a dream.

So judge all my actions, and everything that I have said.
Judge me now my love, and burn me while you still can.
And yes I still remember the feeling of your hand on my shoulder.
I can still remember your soft voice, whispering into my ear.

Hate me because I'm just so fucking worthless.
Forgive me naught, for I am truly just a hopeless bastard.
Judge my actions and everything in my life that I had said.
Never forgive me my love, for I do truly deserve this pain.

"Find me my love, hidden right there - where I've always been..."

Upon the Crescent Moon

His daughter waits for him, upon the crescent moon.
She waits up all night, wondering if father will come home soon.
His daughter waits for him, there upon the crescent moon.
Wondering and wondering, if father will come home soon.

He's on his way home, to hold his daughter in his arms.
He's on his way home, and the journey was indeed long.
He's been gone for some time, still she waits up all night.
He's on his way home, to hold his daughter in his arms.

His daughter waits up for her father, upon the crescent moon.
Her father he's on his way home, hopefully to arrive soon.
She waits up for her father, she waits up for him every night.
Upon the crescent, she waits for father to return home...

Loss Of Reputation

So I am nothing now, just like I've always been.
A fucking waste of existence, ranting on about my sins.
So I lost my reputation, when I said that I've killed God.
So now I am hated, just a fucking waste of life.

So yes I am truly nothing, just like I always have been.
And in my soul can be found, the very definition of torment.
So I guess I'll never drown, I'll just be waiting here at the bottom.
It's true that nobody cares now, so I guess I lost my reputation.

Laugh with me as we pull the trigger, a flash of light and all is quiet.
Weep with me my children, because the game is over and we have lost.
Laugh with me my angry children, because soon we will have our day.
Follow me over the ledge, we'll fall forever and just laugh it all away.

So I'm nothing now, worthless like I always have been.
I'm a pathetic poet, ranting endlessly about my sins.
So I lost some reputation, when I said that it was I that killed God.
But we know the truth, and that is why I will be forever hated.

They Say...

They say that I'm a sadistic sideshow freak.
They say that I am too evil to ever feel love.
They say that I am falling and soon enough I'll reach an end.
They say that I am the Devil, so I guess they're right again.

They say I need to wake up and realize that I'm asleep.
They say I am but a shadow of the man I used to be.
They say that I'm dead now and just trying to remember my life.
They say that I'll always be alone, and again they are right.

They say that I'm a creature, in which does not deserve to feel love.
They say that I need to let go and just hold on to my dreams.
They say that I am dead now, swinging at the end of a rope.
So I guess they were always right, that I would die alone.

On Dire Wishes

Strange feelings as I place the blade beneath my flesh.
Odd that I feel nothing, but a numb whisper upon my nerves.
So I slowly separate, removing my face from my body.
So I laugh, because I haven't seen myself in years.

Screaming upon those dire wishes, of making it passed today.
I've tried my best but was far too weak, that is why I was cast away.
I need now no more drugs, only the pleasure of pure pain.
I have found myself again, funny that I still have nothing to say.

Twisted and shallow, it drives cold beneath the flesh.
Soon enough there will be nothing left of me, and it's for the best.
Weeping upon these dire wishes, of making it passed tomorrow.
So I have to just laugh, because I have again found my face.

I am the demon, the monster, your angel, your salvation.
We are the forgotten, we are unknown to even ourselves.
And it's just so strange that as I cut off my face, I felt nothing.
Truly odd that all I desire, is to feel pain once again.

Partake of the Fruits

Come partake of the fruits of the tree of knowledge.
Come learn the true origin of our creation.
Partake of the fruits and learn that we were meant to be so much more.
Come partake of the fruits so that the truth will be known.

Listen closely to the whisper behind the rhyme.
Follow close as we walk upon the line.
Remember logic and all that it stands for.
Learn the truth of our existence, or soon we will exist no more.

Come partake of the fruits of the tree of knowledge.
Come learn the true history of humans as a species.
Partake of the fruits and learn why it is that they are kept from us.
Come partake of the fruits and relearn that which we have always known.

Cutting Me Out

Cutting me out of my own past.
I guess I never really expected to last.
I need now to get a fucking grip.
I need to let it out, just go ahead and snap.
So then I'll just remain here.
Cutting me out of my own past.
To convince myself that I truly did never exist.
Cutting me out of my own past.
Endlessly flooding my mind with nonsense.
But maybe it was once for a better reason.
Then again maybe not at all.
I guess I never really was a great person.
Then again I might never have been human at all.
So then I'll just continue.
Cutting me out of my own past.
I will continue to be a faded memory.
A forgotten ghost, lost in our forgotten past.

Arts & Massacres

Define it clearly, the shattering of my faith.
Reverse it completely, all of what my heart did say.
Watch real closely, can you see the death of my soul?
Feel all of my torments, and now you too are so cold.

Define us clearly, we are creatures of hatred and death.
It's all so beautiful, as we fill the bloody canvas.
Just look real closely, can you see the death of my soul?
Everything is so beautiful, beautifully dead and never to return.

Take those words now, hold them close with pride.
Define it completely, the twisted shattering of my faith.
Just watch real closely, as I cut off my own face.
Can you feel it now, the true essence of our hatred and rage?

"It's all so beautiful, so very beautiful..."

212

Bleeding Out (One Pill At a Time.)

Long ago, the blade was pushed deep beneath the flesh.
Then it hit the bone, but the pain did never end.
Now all I can hear at night, is constant screaming and weeping.
But I know that I truly am doing it all to myself.

I'm just lying on the floor, screaming and weeping.
Watching as from my wrist, I begin to bleed out the pills of my past.
Still they remain in me, all of the little torments within my head.
So I'm lying on the floor, bleeding out just one pill at a time.

So long ago, her voice was all that I needed.
Now I can no longer remember, if I was ever even alive.
I can feel now only torment, torment of both my heart and mind.
So I remain here on the floor just bleeding out, one pill at a time...

I'm still waiting, to see what it is that God will do with me.
I'm still screaming, weeping alone here so cold on the floor.
But nothing has really changed I say, "*I'm still wandering lost in my mind.*"
Still I'm here bleeding out, only one pill at a time.

Dynamic Resistors

Moving on for miles upon these jagged stones.
Miles upon endless miles exhausting our souls.
And over the years, I know that my world has been changing.
Still we move onward, no matter how bad the pain is.

And over the years, I know that something in me has changed.
Still those forces remain out there, trying to hold me back again.
But I must move passed this now, far passed all of the pains of then.
I cannot let them numb me down, no – not again!

Moving onward like I always have been upon these jagged stones.
Miles upon endless miles I've been moving away from your world.
And over the years, I realized that they have been trying to *hold me back*.
But I must just keep moving onward, far passed the memories of then...

"I can't let them stop me."

Taste - The Fungus?

Taste of the fungus that is burning into my flesh.
Watch as our world melts and nothing of us will be left.
Hold onto me tight, before we all fade away.
Kiss me upon my eyes, so that I can finally see.

We are gone to a much better point of existence.
We are lost and we don't ever want to be found.
We have reached beyond the stars to find.
We are our own Gods and Devils, "*we are nothing but a blink in time.*"

Taste of the fungus that is melting into my flesh.
I think that I'm dying, I think that we are all already dead.
So hold onto me tight my love, for soon we are to fade away.
Kiss me now while you still can, before I'm erased again.

I think that I'm forgotten by the whole world and me.
I feel like I'm a ghost, remembering the bliss of insanity.
I watch as my world is slowly forgotten just like me.
Come taste of the fungus, so that you might remain with me...

Slipstream

Follow into the slipstream and all is fine.
Take of our torment and leave it to fade with time.
Taste of my lips again and you truly do hate me.
Look me in the eyes and just say that I am nothing!

Follow into the slipstream and all will be calm.
Look me in the eyes and then kill me my love.
Take my heart out and just throw it away.
Tell me the truth now, that I was nothing to you but a waste.

Follow me now into the slipstream and just let it all go.
Take of my torments that still remain beneath the snow.
Taste of my hatred and I am but only a shard.
A fragment of the true evil that now infests your soul.

Defying Sentinels

They cannot forever keep me locked in this cage.
They cannot stop me from fucking seizing this day!
They cannot kill me, for I have always been dead.
They cannot control me for I am the master of the thoughts in my head.

Now I'm fighting to be there, the hero in the end.
I am fighting to save the world, before we burn for all our sins.
I am fighting to survive this, pointless war of our mortal souls.
I will forever fight, to save this dying world...

They cannot contain me for I am everywhere.
They cannot destroy me for I am always and shall exist forever.
They cannot stop me from saving this world from itself.
They cannot defeat me, for I have already won...

I shall defy these sentinels, for it is in my nature.
I shall save us all, before this story truly ends.
I am the hero, in which no one ever believed in.
I shall stand and fight, to save our dying freedoms...

"So come now and join me."

Fuck My Thoughts!

Fuck my thoughts, I guess I don't really matter.
Fuck my dreams, because they seem too difficult.
Fuck my hopes, I guess that I'm just out of luck.
Fuck my world and existence, fuck me and my thoughts.

I have tried my hardest, to not grab you by your throat.
I have tried my hardest to not laugh as you choke.
I have looked into your eyes, and then they went dark.
I have laughed at your death, as I ripped out your heart.

Fuck all of my thoughts, I guess that I am insane.
Fuck all of what I am and everything that I say.
Fuck all of my entire existence, my hopes and my dreams.
Fuck me and my thoughts, "come to think of it, fuck everything!!!"

A Much Better Taste

It's a much better taste, rolling over the tip of my tongue.
It is a much better way, to just pull the trigger of the gun.
It was a mistake that we made, when we admitted our love.
It was my greatest leap of faith, when I told you we were done.

Must it always be this way, so Goddamn cold and lonely?
Must I always feel this pain, here inside my broken heart?
Must you tell me that I'm worthless, every time that we meet?
Must our story truly end this way, on such a bitter taste..?

It's a much better taste now rolling over the tip of my tongue.
It was so much fun I say, when we pulled that thread and come undone.
It is a much better leap of faith, as I begin to step over this ledge.
It is a much better ends, to a story of our eternal love.

Must it always end this way, so Goddamn cold and tragic?
Must we always part this way, *you leaving me with your knife in my back?*
Must we say what it is that we say, *could we maybe pretend that all is fine?*
Must we admit that our love is dead? *Now passed away like a bittersweet taste.*

Because We Loved

Sharpened fingernails ripping into our twisted hearts.
Of a time left in splinters, with tragic memories torn apart.
Lips that shall always haunt me, her words echo on within.
Reminding me of that time, when this war did begin...

Because I loved you, that is why you are now dead.
Because you loved me, that is why our world did end.
Because we were happy, all the Gods in heaven were outraged.
Because we loved each other, that is why we were torn away...

Now left in splinters, tattered memories in a forgotten book.
Time has taken it toll, but still demands more than what it already took.
Of our love that is dead, by the hands of both God and fate.
It is because we loved each other that we are now in our graves.

"Fuck this fate – For I shall always cherish what little time we had..."

"But a Child."

Nothing but a child, weeping alone in pain.
Nothing but a child, bleeding alone and in shame.
Nothing but a demon, growing within an innocent soul.
Nothing but destruction, now infesting this world.

As the skies all darken, here at high noon.
Our lives are left to wither, all of our hopes now doomed.
For death is coming and we cannot deny him.
So smile with me, for we all truly deserve this.

Was nothing but a hero, which failed to save the day.
Was nothing but a hopeless dreamer in which never could sleep.
Was nothing but a poet, trying to describe his heart.
Was nothing but a child left bleeding alone, torn apart.

And as this entire world it freezes, I have only to laugh.
As all that I had ever loved, now it is all dead.
Was there maybe a chance, that I could have saved us at all?
I was just far too weak to save us, "for I was nothing but a child..."

Felt-Heartbreaks

The glass spilt over and now a lingering stain.
Shards of my past, beneath layers and layers of paint.
And it is hatred, which reminds me to just let go.
Of that forgotten love, left there under the snow.

And with time maybe, I can release some of the pain.
With time it might all be forgotten, just erased away.
Like all that I have said to her, when we held each other close.
And just maybe someday, the sun shall rise again.

Upon that dire thought of regaining some of my past.
Now I'm left in the wonder, of if we can ever go back.
Then again it causes, only more torment and pain.
I have felt again the heartbreak, of knowing the truth.

My love is dead, she is dead and never to return...

Sickness Of Our Times

Let's turn our minds back and remember all those lies.
Let us try to believe in them once again, but this time not in spite.
Just try to remember what it was like to feel true love in your heart.
Remember what it was like to but be looking into the eyes of death.

Let us go back now to a time when darkness controlled all.
A time when we held the answers with no questions to ask.
Remember the path we had chosen which led into the abyss.
Let's try to remain there, within our pasts, when we were happy...

Can you follow then, as so tormented by the sickness of our times?
There it goes again and now we're wandering about so blind.
Just try to remember all of which was said in those days.
Can then we perhaps survive this, the world we did make.

Let us venture back now, back to this present time of dismay.
Let us hold onto these moments, let's survive this war everyday.
And we shall hold onto the questions, for all answers have been found.
Remember that we must only survive, this sickness of our times...

Hidden Within Her Flesh

That lost key, found hidden behind her eyes.
That moment when we had touched, a part of my heart did die.
There was a time when all I had wanted was to kiss her lips.
But then I had realized that all along I have been dead.

Just a ghost un-remembered, wishing I could say...
Then even if I had, nothing would have changed.
But I like to think, that maybe someday it might.
But all still remains hidden, behind those blue eyes.

So on I go, losing all of my strength and breath.
And I know that my heart still remains hidden within her flesh.
But she moves on still, because I've all along been dead.
But I like to think that maybe someday, I just might awake...

"What Of Logic?"

What of logic is now left for us to save?
Have we any hope here, at the bottom of our graves?
This is truly a disgrace, what it is we have become.
There is no turning back now, the bullet has already left the gun...

So what of logic now, I guess we never did care.
What of our hearts and souls, burning alone in despair.
We have done this all to ourselves, the destruction of our minds.
What of hope now, as we have all crossed the line?

Then taken far passed the emotions called fear and rage.
Eyes open then to learn, upon that next turning page.
For waves of nonsense, crashing against our minds.
Then we are to know, that we're running out of time.

So what then of logic is left now for us to save?
Are we ever to learn, as we lie here at the bottoms of our graves?
So tell me then, have we any hope to be saved?
What has become of our logic, lying there in our graves...?

Fuck Conformity!

Stand in line, and then all together follow.
Into the darkness, of numbed thoughts and tragic lives.
Stand now together, so that we can burn as one.
Do as you are told and be but another blind servant to their needs.

Fuck conformity and all who follow its lead.
Be but only yourself, if there is still a self for you to be.
Stand tall and speak your voice, so that you are recognized.
Be yourself and live your life for - you...

Now projected far passed the thoughts of conventionality.
Led to believe that tomorrow shall indeed rise and save the day.
Follow along into the darkness if that is what you wish.
Or maybe you might want to follow me, stand tall and say "fuck conformity!"

Serenaded By Demons

Her voice rings numb as the sun in the sky is leaving.
All beneath the surface of the scars still remain bleeding.
But then she starts weeping, all alone there screaming.
What have I to say as she just lies there alone, still weeping?

Will it comfort her, to be serenaded by demons?
Will I ever find the correct way to reach our ending?
Have I not then to say, that I do truly love you?
I shall remain here for all time, for you to return to...

So I sing my songs but have they made their way to you my love?
So I sing on and on, hoping that I might hold you once more.
So is it helping at all, these emotions which I've been beseeching?
Is it at all comforting you, being serenaded by demons?

Her voice rings numb as all the star-lights are fleeting.
All within her mind, left dire hopes of our hearts still bleeding.
But then she starts weeping, all alone out here just weeping.
So what have I to say to the *angel*, for I am nothing more than a *demon*?

Abjured

I'm ready now to say that I've had enough.
I'm ready now to just throw it all away.
I'm ready to say that I feel nothing.
I am ready to just end my love for you today.

It is over now like it always has been.
We are further now, from ever realizing our dreams.
I am done with all of this, constant wars of my mind.
I'm ready to let you go my love, ready now to say goodbye.

I am ready, to just say that I'm done with my heart.
I am ready now, to rip it out and tear it apart!
I am done with all of this torment, of love itself.
I am done with this life, and ready now to just step away....

Over the Corpse

As I stand over the corpse, I question only why is it wearing my face.
As I look upon the gravestone, why is it that it reads my name?
As I'm standing here over the corpse, in my head I wonder why!
As I am now that corpse lying in the ground, looking up at the sky.

Have I anything more to state at this time, other than those screams!
Taken unknown upon our dead yet unending dreams.
Then sorrow weeps and she waits not for another moment.
So have now this corpse anything left, other than rage?!

As I look to my past, I know now that I was always dead.
As I reach into my heart, I have found but only tar.
As what point is there to be made through all of this?
As I am now standing over myself, I have but only to laugh...

With arms reaching deeper into my forgotten past.
Voices echoing the truth of the murder on that day.
Eyes open to that fact in which we cannot throw away.
So I have but only to laugh, at my own dead face...

Exciting Actions

Photos taken on that day.
To remind ourselves of the pain.
Troubles felt all that day.
To make us feel guilty in the eyes of God.

Is it not good enough a reason for our world to burn?
Was not treason but soon you'll learn?
With our minds open and bleeding into the abyss.
Watch real closely or it'll all be missed.

Photos taken on that day.
Pictures to remind us of the pains.
Troubles aching with our hearts all day.
So now I am sorry, that it was you I couldn't save.

Seriously Bleeding

Years ago, she cut into my chest and left me bleeding.
Now what is left here in my dreaming?
Have I still it in my heart to love her always?
As still to this day, I'm seriously bleeding.

Nothing now left of my heart to regain.
I am a lonely demon, weeping in shame.
But upon that thought I had filled myself with pride.
And from that day on, just constant wars of this mind.

Years ago, she kissed my lips and told me to hold on.
I held on forever, as I watched our world decay.
Years ago she had said that she loved me.
So I guess that truly "I" was her greatest mistake.

For nothing of me now can be saved or regained.
I am a lonely demon, an outcast with no face.
But upon those passed dreams that had filled us with bliss.
Still to this day I am seriously bleeding *from the open wound in my chest.*

Upon the Asphalt

Blood drops dripping upon the asphalt.
Ages speaking within these bones.
Time left now all about in splinters.
Dust to ash, ashes from these bones.

Blood dripping upon the asphalt.
Hatred growing within my mind.
Darkness looming all across this land.
Death was found beneath my grave.

As the blood drops are dripping upon the asphalt.
From my cut open eye bleeds out all of me.
In time they might all begin to understand it.
But for now it's a secret held between you and me...

Complaints

Truth of life now taken and broken.
Love felt burning, deep in torment.
I am screaming so loud, but no one can hear.
The truth is that I do love you, but I just can't say...

So take my hand, please kill me now!
Words untaken, as we fall down – down – down.
For faith of our destruction, I am the one who fell...
Fuck me and everything, both my heaven and my hell.

Please come and take me, far-far from here.
Please just love me, wipe away all my tears.
Just fucking say it! That I am unloved and damned.
So the truth is that I am worthless.
I am worthless, "*fucked and damned...*"

Decades More to Go...

Watch as this poet inks another decade into this page.
Watch as the blood flows from my eyes and onto her grave.
Look real closely at the scars on both my hands and my lips.
Can you not see the truth of the pain, which has made me into this..?

Decades more to go, before I'll be able to just let it all go.
Somehow between now and then, I shall end this world, again and again!
Just to watch it burn, just so that I might someday learn from my pain.
Still so long to go, before we can close the book and forget this page.

Watch as this poet describes the fact that I once again do feel love.
Watch as I bleed out all of what it is that makes me who I am.
Look inside of my pains to see that tomorrow won't change a thing.
Still decades more to go, before they erase all of what I say...

Just a little more to go, then I will be in her arms.
Just three little words to speak and I'll be in her heart.
My muse laughing, as I lie here screaming all alone.
Decades more to go, then maybe I'll be okay with being alone.
As she burns all of my pages and my pains away.

Chapter 13

Between Flesh & Bone

25 Pointless Years

Drowning in an ocean of blood and tears.
Describing these pains for so many pointless years.
Trying my best but still I constantly fail.
Although you may be my angel, still this is my hell.

For on turns the blades now, seeping into the wrist.
Softly spoken truths, so then sadly they are missed.
So what of this emotion which has already driven me this far?
Can you taste the acid in my blood, can you see it's become but tar?

So on I go weeping and screaming and bleeding and fleeting!
Waiting for the moment when God tells me that it's time.
Time to just let it go and to step towards the light.
I am waiting still, here in darkness out of sight.

For all of my life, I've been drowning in an ocean of blood and tears.
Trying my best to describe to you all of my pains and fears.
So read real close and find the truth hidden between each line.
Of the 25 pointless years of this poet's life...

Lost In a Crowd

Stepping upon these unknown faces.
Watching as our time is constantly wasted.
Feeling as if I'm out of place still.
Knowing that there is no more hope.
For love of hatred and endless torment.
Felt as I reach out and into the light.
What of all these twisted moments?
When all I want is to open my eyes.
"To see her standing right next to me."
Then I realize that I am lost in my own sanity.
Damn these endless amounts of pointless faces.
But none of them are the one that I seek.
Someday I just hope to find it.
The thing in which shall set me free.
Until then I will wander lost in this crowd.
Lost and searching for what can never be found.
"That one soul, which truly loves me..."

Leave No Tread

Step lightly upon the face of your God.
Cut into its heart and awake now lost.
Reach out and into the flames of hell.
Leave no tread and all shall remain at peace.

For as the sentence is stated backwards.
Then the mirrored image throws it off.
What then shall be held in our hearts?
The answer must be, nothing at all.

So step real lightly as you wander through the dark.
Remember what the Devil had then said.
But you never did listen from the start.
Just leave no tread or you shall be found.

Then running endlessly away from the stress.
Cutting into your God and raping what it said.
There must be a purpose to the truth of our death.
Leave no tread, step real light, and hold your breath.

"The end is here..."

Psychosis Defined

Screaming at my reflection, but it tells me that I'm okay.
Lusting an angel's nightmares, upon another twist of fate.
Trying to find some hope still, but only sorrow can be found.
Still cutting deep into myself, just seeking a better way to get out.

Does this matter anymore at this fucked up point in time?
Am I still the same person that loved her, once upon a time?
Is there any chance for, us to reach salvation beyond this pain?
Am I still the man in which you loved, or have I truly gone insane?

As I am screaming at the moon now, begging her to take me back.
I am reaching into the abyss, to slit open the Devil's wrists.
I am what I've always been, and I need to escape this cage!
So I guess I understand what it is that I am, "a man in which cannot be saved."

As it Hits the Floor

Fire dripping into the lost fragments of our past.
Again upon another ending and I just hope this one lasts.
But maybe I'm just bitching, because it helps me to sleep.
But I'm still awake, and this world is still but a dream.

Then as her words fall gentle upon my heart.
The thoughts of her loving me, it tears me apart.
So I do believe that I'm just gonna rant on and on the same.
For this is my world, my heaven and hell that I made.

And as God tells me to just give it time and pray.
I pray for the ending to hurry and come today.
Then as she remembers, that I am but only a way to pass time.
It all goes again the same, and we mix it with the lime.

Liquid fire dripping into the forgotten fragments of our past.
This blood tastes like wine, yet someone spilt the glass.
So then it shatters and all love and hope, it hits the floor.
So then she comes and whispers to me, that she loves me no more.

"Come join me to see, the death of our dreams..."

Solitude & Ignorant

It is dark here, within the back of my troubled mind.
I've had enough of this shit, for time after time after time after time!
So get the fuck away, and let me die here on my own.
I don't care what might be out there, "someone waiting on me..."

I've fought for so damn long, and shall remain alone for eternity.
So just let me be forgotten, don't stand there and act like you care.
I am now what was made of me, just another sad sideshow freak!
I don't want to know what could happen, I just want to be erased.

It is so dark here, within my fucked up troubled mind.
It is so cold here, lost and forgotten in the sands of time.
So just forget me, for I did never truly exist.
Leave me to be forgotten, here with in my decaying abyss.

"Good For You..."

Good for you, I'm glad that you have found your way.
Good for you, I'm so happy that you've been saved.
Good for you, I am glad that you have now what you want.
Good for you, I'm so happy that you have won...

There it is given, all the bitter hopes of our dismay.
And come to think of it, I just hope they understand what I mean.
Of the horror that remains here, feasting upon our souls.
I hope you understand, what you've been told.

Good for you, I am glad that you've won the day.
Good for you, I am so happy that you were saved.
Good for you, I am grateful that you're no longer alone.
Good for you, I am so happy that you found a place to call home...

Then on goes the turning of the gears of fate.
So we tried to hold on forever, but then we fell away.
I was but only trying my best, to just be here for you.
But I am truly happy, that your love came back too.
Good for you...

Respected BullShit

Speak of those lies which still try to remain.
Take of the drug that is poisoning my brain.
Laugh at the picture of the dead child's face.
Step forward off the ledge and then we are free.
Backwards dreaming upon these endless strives.
Preaching respected bullshit just to pass some time.
Remembering what it feels like to taste of the flesh.
Blood dripping off my teeth and I love that best.
Of a dire fate that is still waiting to commence.
Spoken of that twisted logic which now makes sense.
Then we are all taken down there where no one can see.
We all have destroyed our lives and are now so weak.
Just hoping that tomorrow might come and end all this pain.
But then we come to remember that tomorrow was yesterday.
So we speak now of this bullshit because we have nothing else to say.

Grinded to the Bone

Fucking torment grinding in me, breaking my heart and taking my breath.
Rage and anguish still define me, nothing I can do will stop this.
Just tear these memories from my head, then I'll laugh as she keeps stabbing me.
Fueling these nightmares of my past, darkness consumes all of me now.
There's nothing I can do to end this, kill the memories of you!

So I am suffocating in torment, feeling as if I'm gonna die.
Put your hand onto my chest, then laugh with me as I cry.
Watch real closely while I am burning, please help me now to open my eyes!
For I can't see a fucking thing now, only the endless darkness of my life!!!

Yes I wake in torment and then see it, it's fucking eating at my mind!
I wake in hell now Oh God I feel it, the acid dripping down my spine!
I wake to see it, all the demons feasting, on my fucked up twisted mind!
I wake and know it, yes God I know it, that I fucking ran out of time!
I wake to nothing, yes I am nothing, but a fucking waste of life!
I speak to - all, of the - voices, screaming inside, of my mind!
I reach out now, to you my love, but you cannot save me!
As all of my world is grinding to nothing, then hidden between flesh and bone!!!

Vampires Know Me

Yes they know me, for I too am the damned.
Yes I've lived for ages, tormented by the pains of my sins.
Yes they do want me, to join in their lustful games.
Yes I am nothing, nothing but evil, pain and rage.

So is it true that my love did insist on me staying?
Is it true that I once had a chance to save the both of us?
Is it possible for me to go back and change this outcome?
Is there any possible way for you to say that you can again love me?

Yes the vampires know me, for I am no different from them.
Yes the Devil wants me, for I do have more power than him.
Yes the vampires need me, to join in their blood-lusts and rage.
Yes I am but a demon, *the demon with angel wings.*
I am damnation and yes, you cannot save me...

Fucking Cinch!

Retracing this tattered past into the darkness of the truth.
Remembering the horror of what it is that I had done to you.
By trying my best to leave something more for you to cherish.
I never meant to hurt you my love and I know you'll never forgive me.

So watch real closely as I begin to destroy this world.
Laugh with me so franticly as now we all burn.
Look into the flames my love, can you see paradise?
We are all burning my love, burning in hell until the end of time...

As then all was so much of a greater cause, a dying grim fact.
It was in our natures, to rip off the angel's wings and then to laugh.
Yet somehow or another it has all boiled down to this fate.
Now we must battle this moment, straight to the grave.

Can then the answers come and take us so very far from here.
As upon that time when we had loved each other ever so dear.
It haunts us still, all of the memories that just won't leave.
So we pull the trigger to find us a little release in this....
But we know now what it is that we must do.
And it's gonna be a fucking cinch!

Distraught

They are reaching into my heart again.
There was truly nothing left to be had.
She was telling me that I meant so much to her.
She had taken my thoughts and burned them again.

Now what have I, only these pains behind my eyes?
So what have I, now only the option to wither and die?
What in the hell have I, left to keep me going through this pain?
What is left of us now, and will we ever find our way?!

They had reached into my heart and found only death.
They had told me I meant so much but then they burned me *away again.*
She was my muse, my guiding light so I'd never be lost.
But she is gone now, and I am left here alone and distraught...

232

Speeding Slowly

It all goes so much faster, when we turn off the lights.
We both see but only, the pleasures of *the night.*
We are now speeding slowing, until we're both satisfied.
She screams as loud as she wants, endless through the night.

It all seems strange as we watch the horizon melt away.
It all feels like heaven, when she ends up getting her way.
There seems to be something, driving us beyond our minds.
So now we are speeding slowly, *laughing as we look our deaths in the eye.*

It all goes much faster, when I let her have her way.
It all feels so great, as all through the night she screams.
We are now speeding so slowly, time itself begins to stop.
If for only a moment, that perfect moment, *"come and gone..."*

Eating The Stars

She flings her arms about, as she dances around in circles.
She reaches to the heavens, together we both howl at the moon.
She is speaking now, of our deaths with Mother Nature.
She is eating of the stars, as she dances with the moon.

She was forever waiting, for her chance to be the one.
She had wanted me to be there, I tried my best but failed.
She was my broken angel, which I never could save.
She was so damn amazing, she was *my love* that fate took away.

She flings her arms about, as she dances around in circles.
She reaches to the heavens, alone now I howl at the moon.
She has already spoken, of our ends with Mother Nature.
She is eating of the stars, as she dances with the moon.

"In the heavens dances, my broken angel..."

Beyond the Playground

Time falls back again into the bitter truth of the cause.
Words unspoken of that chapter burnt away like the pains.
It comes now to this last dire chance of making that point.
For all along I have had so damn much on my mind to say.

As then all the pains go tripping far beyond the playground.
Visions of the past so darkened dulled lifeless and gloom.
As within our hatreds we learn that we have found our way.
To erase the torments of the past, these memories of rage.

For as time falls back again and brings us to the truths of the cause.
The grim fate of our dreams left then burnt shattered and lost.
It comes down to this last dire chance of making that point.
And still I have so damn much left on my mind to say.

As there it is to be of our grim nightmares of the past.
Beyond the playground lies those hidden memories of rage and death.
But it all means something more of what has at this point been said.
Beyond the playground shall be found that hidden truth of the past.

Destroying Matter

I am once again destroying this world which I had made.
I am killing each and every worthless little bastard that gets in my way.
I am once again destroying matter and all which exists in creation.
I am destroying everything in which I have loved in my life...

There it goes all breaking, decaying into *nothing* so that it can reflect me.
All of this world it is over, so time for us to just laugh and to scream!
There we go all drowning, drowning in the roaring flames of hell.
All that we have ever loved, it is gone and never to return...

I am once again destroying this world in which I had made.
I am killing each and every soul that stands in my way - so worthless and weak.
I am once again destroying this whole universe and my every creation.
I have now destroyed, everything I had loved in my life...

234

I Know You're Faking!

Into those beautiful eyes fall all of my undying hopes and fears.
She proves it without a doubt that I have been dead for so many years.
She told me that I was but *dreaming* and that I still had a chance to *awake.*
Then I had to let it all go, because I knew her love for me was fake.

She tried her best to make that point, that I am already gone and buried.
She tried to hold me while in the flames of hell I was burning.
She was the only one that knew the gravity of my bitter dismay.
She had then left that scar on my lips, and still the pain won't dissipate.

As into her beautiful eyes fall all of my unending rants of hope and rage!
She had proven *without a doubt* that I am but a forgotten page of the past.
But I know that she was faking, all the love for me that she had.
I am at this point so tired, so please just burn me away.

"Still I fall forever, into those beautiful Eyes..."

Her Aching Scars

Gently I run my tongue along her aching scars.
She begins to whimper as we lie together - alone in the dark.
She grabs my face and then places her tongue into my mouth.
Together we are alone, so gently rubbing all of her aching scars.

Time has all but stopped for us at this particular moment.
She digs her fingernails into my flesh and then grips my spine.
She wants to feel that pleasure, of the numbness yet to be.
She digs deeper inside and then takes my soul away from me.

Gently I run my tongue along all of her aching scars.
She lets out a soft whimper as we lie together - alone in the dark.
She put my hands around her waist as together our pains slowly fade.
Together we are alone, still gently rubbing her aching scars.
"Cherishing the pain, as we together drift away."

Easy But Not Cheap

It was so easy to rip my heart out and just throw it away.
It was so very pointless and no one has ever cared for this poet's pains.
All of these voices scream still, reminding us of the reasons.
It was so very easy to destroy my life, but still you wish not to see.

Of the bitter truth that hides the agony within these bones.
Of that dire fate that keeps us here so broken and alone.
For there is no better reasons of the fact of our unending torments.
For there is now only this last statement of our grim ends.

It was so easy to just watch as my love had walked away.
It was so very easy to end my life with your sharpened blade.
All of these statements might mean something more to her eyes.
It was easy but not cheap, to sell my soul to save her life.

"Here in hell I smile, for she lives on in peace..."

Dilapidated

Within this hourglass that remains stuck in my mind.
Here I decay eternal, time after time after time after time...
Then as the sands begin to slow and the last grain falls upon my face.
I am now but an element, I am the true epitome of death and decay.
Here I am locked within the hourglass that remains stuck in my mind.
I try my best to break myself out, "Get me out of this cage!!!"
Time is all I am left with now, nothing at all of my soul to remain.
Here I lie within the hourglass, locked within myself in eternal decay.
"God take my words now and give to them the means."
Watch as I fight to break myself out of this damned mental cage!
Can then you see it as the truth burns within my eyes.
Can you save us and then smile as together we are both killing time.
Then we laugh at the irony that I have all along waited.
Waited for the time to come, when we together reach the end of time.
Here and now is what I've awaited.
Smile with me as we together laugh and kill time...

Feeding The Dogs

With that rusted nail you are digging.
Digging in deep so that you can get at my brain.
In ages it has gone and on and on and on unspoken.
Open my mind now to see what it is that hides between sanity and me.

Then they are fueling my every motive to the grave.
Then they all but laugh as we together burn away.
They are the voices that for ages have been screaming in my mind.
And to you "my love" I've been speaking, but I know "you" don't exist.

So what am I, "tell me now because I need the comfort!?"
So what have I, "left in my life that makes me a human!?"
So what then to say, "as we drift further apart and deeper into hell!?"
So can we please, "forget that this whole world did ever exist!?"

With that rusted nail you have been digging.
Digging for ages trying your best to get at my brain.
We had together reached this moment and we find our souls are lost.
We had but frittered them away, we fed them to the dogs...

"Keep trying your very best, to get at my brain..."

Swallow My Shames

Reach into the shadows and find that missing piece.
Look into your heart now and forget the pointless means.
Of the breaking of the life that just sadly could not be.
Reach into the darkness and there is truly where you shall find me.

Her eyes were indeed beautiful, so cold that they destroyed my heart.
Her lips were so electrifying, a shock every time that we kissed.
Her words meant so much to me, now I can just barely remember.
Her eyes took a hold of me, then they just threw me away.

Reach into the shadows and find that question in which you seek.
Look into your heart and know that it must still bleed.
Out all of the anger and hatred that is felt when I'm close.
I do my best to swallow my shames and admit that I am but a ghost.

Cloudless

For ages I've been falling from the heavens.
For ages I've known only the knowledge of defeat.
For endless amounts of times this soul has been slain.
For ages I've been falling, deeper into the hell that I made.

What then of misery that binds us to our graves.
Maybe it's that look in the child's eyes, as it begins to rain.
So take of those memories and remove them from my head.
Leave me to be dead and un-remembered, for that is what I am.

Pain is all that is left to remain of those bitter resurrections.
Sorrow is felt pumping through my veins day after day.
Laughter is all that has been fueling me, such sweet insanity and rage.
The end has been searching for me, and then we awake at the start.

For ages I've been falling from the heavens above.
For ages I've been falling through the beautiful cloudless skies.
For so much of this war has passed and we have found only bloodshed.
For so many ages I've been falling, just waiting until I can awake again...

"Falling through beautiful cloudless skies..."

A Lot to Say...

Decades passed and still I do have a lot to say.
I'm not even halfway through yet.
This is still but a prelude of the wars yet to be.
I have said so much at this point, and still I have a lot to say...

The paint it drips down lightly it spills upon her lips.
She remembers how it tastes, our one and final kiss.
We had fought so hard to not lose each other.
Then we succeeded only in losing ourselves.

Decades passed and yes I do still have much more to say.
I'm telling you right now, that this isn't even halfway.
We are but at a prelude of the wars that are yet to be.
I have said so much over the years, and still I have a lot to say...

Beneath the Eyelid

Frozen teardrops bleeding out and they fall beneath the eyelids.
Her broken heart is lost and we can never again find it.
Our story has ended and no one is left that can remember.
Of that time of war, and all the truths found just beneath her eyelids.

They all seem to know now, even if they don't truly believe it.
We are all burning in hell now, and I know that we deserve this.
There is no chance to get out, and see what just might have been.
I know that I could just dream forever, of that life that could not be.

Frozen teardrops falling down and they shattered upon the stone.
Her broken heart is lost, her whole body is freezing cold.
Our paths have parted, and now we are so very far away.
We are still at war though, we are fighting ourselves still to this day...

They say that there is no chance in saving this world we had made.
We are all together damned and in hell we shall forever stay.
There is no hope, we have searched for peace but could not find it.
The truths all behind these wars, *they shall be found just beneath her eyelids.*

Freebasing Ink

Sanity dissolves away within the whipping flames.
Agony has become a pleasure and such a twisted game.
Evil is all that remains of that once innocent mind.
Hatred, passion and rage are all that I have left to feel inside.

The ink it is pumping all throughout my decaying veins.
Death gropes my heart as the smoke takes my breath away.
The Devil is watching close and waiting for his chance.
God is up there just laughing, at all of my pointless rants.

With my sanity goes the feeling of ever knowing love.
Agony has become my life and all that I am today.
Evil is the best way to define me, I am hatred, I am rage.
The ink it is what makes me, the forgotten ghost that I am today.

"I am the ink that bleeds-out my poetry..."

239

Deafen

Hollow weeping the night into the grave.
Mindless digging into my skull to tear out my brain.
Deafened heartbeats felt numb inside my chest.
And of our pointless love, I loved most the end.

Endlessly lost and weeping the night into the grave.
Mindlessly wishing that I could awake from this unending pain.
Deafened screams go on haunting my every lonely thought.
And I miss most the feeling, her holding me so very tight.

Blind I had seen as the light burned my soul and destroyed my faith.
Mindless I think of only the truth that lies waiting in my grave.
Deafened heartbeats felt numb as she places her hand onto my chest.
And of our failed attempt at love, I miss most her soft kiss...

Hollow weeping all my nights into the grave.
Mindless I wait to see the ending of this world of pain.
Deafened voices still echoing on far passed my death.
And of our pointless love, I loved most the end.

Backwards Prayers

I speak of that emotion as my blood drains.
I pray for forgiveness yet I believe it to be all in vain.
I reach out and feel nothing as the coldness takes its grip.
My eyes roll back and I laugh upon my end.

I speak with God and the Devil and they say that all is fine.
I pray to be forgiven for each of my mortal crimes.
I reach out to feel something but I feel nothing now at all.
My eyes they slowly open and I awake bloody on the floor.

I speak of that emotion of feeling so cold and drained.
I pray that you never have to endure any of these pains.
I reach out to you yet I feel not a thing at my fingertips.
My eyes they are open now and I laugh upon our end...

Alive Under the Floor

I buried my love, alive under the floor.
I saw what was waiting behind that open door
I buried my love to be with her forevermore.
I know she's awake down there, alive under the floor.

She was all that I had ever wanted.
She was my world and my life.
She was the only thing that I ever needed.
She was everything to me and more.

Yes I know she is waiting for me, alive under the floor.
My love is waiting, still waiting, waiting for me to return.
I had buried my love, to keep her safe in this decaying world.
I know my love is safe down there, alive under the floor...

Screaming Mental

Small blades seeping into my brain and causing me to freak!
Sharp little needles digging into my eyes to control what I see!
Odd voices screaming mental within my dying mind!
On and on goes the feasting of the demons upon my sanity!

So tear into my body and find that which to seek!
Find that missing piece of the riddle that goes in reverse!
Know of the mental struggle that makes us who we are!
Scream at the sight and truth that we did this to ourselves!

Small blades bleeding out of my eyes as I weep in pain!
Sharp little needles still they are digging so deep into my brain!
Odd voices screaming mental here in my dying mind!
On and on and on and on goes the torment down my spine!

See that we are the reasons as to why this world burns!
Feel as the flames take us to that place beyond the clouds!
Know that we are nothing but a failed dream of hope!
Scream with us mental as we bathe in the flames of hell..!

Find My Blanket!

Find my blanket and give to me comfort.
Find my heart and put it back into my chest.
Save me "Mother" for I am now falling.
Falling into the abyss of the nightmare that is reality!

Find my blanket and comfort all of my fears.
Keep me safe and in your arms with loving care.
Save me "Mother" because it is dark and I cannot see.
Wake me from this nightmare and take me back to our dream.

Find my blanket to keep me comforted and at peace.
Find my mind and place it back into my head.
Save me "Mother" for I am now falling.
I have awakened on the floor, "fell out of my bed."

Find my broken heart and put it back into my chest.
Find my blanket and give my mind some rest.
Please just take the time, please save me "Mother!"
Give me my blanket, comfort me, "I am so cold"...

Let's Smoke It Away

Let's take of those memories and smoke them away.
Let's take of our identities and erase them away.
Let's forget who we are to ease ourselves of the pain.
Let's take of our past and just smoke it all away.

Is this the mask that you hide behind your face?
Am I that dreamer that is still fucking awake!
Are we the ones that will reach out far passed the stars?
Is it at all likely for us to someday remember who we are!?

Let's take of our memories and smoke it all away.
Let's take up poetry and then erase the truth of our fates.
Let's take that step now just smoke it all away.
Let's forget to remember that we had smoked our lives away...

This I've Awaited

This I've awaited for so many countless years.
The coming of the end of these wars of pain.
This I've awaited for so many countless years.
The passing of our lives and then all is quiet and at peace.

This day has been coming and I am glad it is here.
Within my own hell I've been waiting, year after year.
Like an apocalypse it had come and we could not stop it.
The end is finally here, and it is this that I've awaited.

Time now to just watch as all is coming to an end.
Time now to get some rest and be ready for the next page.
Time then for us to remember, of the paths that we've lain.
Time for us to accept the ending, to move on, *"it is this I've awaited."*

Drinking (The Neon Questions.)

Smashing my head against a bloody headstone.
Drinking of the Neon questions as I scream through the night.
Of the rage of being a tired and enraged musician.
The rage of being a poet that had now opened his eyes.

I see the truth that lies hidden there behind the page.
I see the questions to the answers that echo in her brain.
I see the ending has now started and we are laughing all the same.
I see that you are dead my love, and I can't even remember your name.

Smashing my head against a bloody headstone.
Drinking of the Neon questions that are hidden within these bones.
Of the rage of being a tormented demon.
The pleasures of being an artwork of a poet's soul...

I am drowning in the Neon questions.
I am awaking now and I see the truth.
I am at the start of a new sort of ending.
I am here within your mind so that we are never alone.

Tilted Upwards

The bottom of my glass now tilted upwards.
The thoughts in my head are making me nauseous.
The burn of the whiskey keeping me grounded.
The sky it falls downwards as I ascend into the heavens.

All of my thoughts are left in fucking splinters.
Her voice it haunts me and *I FUCKING WANT IT TO END*!!!!
This mind it is gone and hopeless, not to be saved.
My heart it is unremembered and left bleeding in pain.

Still I wait for her to tell me, what it is that made her love me.
Still I ask the same damn questions, of why did I fail at our love?
Still I want that Goddamn answer, I *FUCKING* need it now!
Still I want you to know, that I did this all for you...

The bottom of my glass now tilted upwards.
Then my body goes downward falling and broken in pain.
The thought of losing you again if yet only in my dreams.
The sky it has fallen, we are all dead my love.
"We are dead and at peace..."

Brightness Consumes

Angels provoke me as they weep upon the line.
Death takes its hold of me, then I smile as we turn off the lights.
The monsters all fear me, for I am the evil of our world.
Look into my eyes and see the fate of you and me.

Angels provoke me as they step over the line.
Demons they all fear me for I am Death itself.
The creatures in my head are all ready to feast.
The taste of the *Angel's* blood, tastes so damn sweet.

Brightness consumes all of my twisted mind.
As darkness retreats back into my heart.
They want me to be more than just a monster.
So now I am the Devil, and I am tearing you apart.

Smiles Upon the Tongue

Smiles upon the tongue as our world it melts away.
Fate did load the gun and still we remain blood-stained.
With hatred defining all the love that I once held for you.
Smiles upon the tongue, as we watch our endings bloom.

This is the place where forgotten souls remain.
This is the logic that can never be replaced.
This is the shadows, the reflection of our dead world.
This is the conclusion, and we did never learn.

With fate still calling me to watch as my love is killed.
Ages upon ages of waiting On-top that Hill.
Looking down with smiles upon my tongue as we are burning.
Then I open my eyes, awake I see a better day.

Smiles upon her tongue as she was waiting.
Waiting for our torment to just hurry up and fade.
And together we watch as we are all melting away.
Smile with us here at the conclusion, of their world of pain.

Thriving In Smoke

All of my past has been burnt away.
I am thriving in the smoke, I am laughing in the flames.
Watching those memories of our love become but a waste.
Here I remain thriving in smoke, as all of us is burnt away.

So I inhale the smoke so that it can get me high.
I inhale the smoke so that it can cloud my troubled mind.
I exhale the pains and torments of my tattered youth.
I exhale all of that pain that was felt between me and you.

All of our photos and my artworks have been burnt away.
I am thriving in the smoke, I am still laughing here in the flames.
I've been watching as the memory of our love becomes but a waste.
Here I shall remain thriving in smoke, here so high in my grave...

"We are somehow thriving, here in these beautiful flames."

"1999"

Simply put, I never thought that I'd be doing this for decades.
Simply put, I have created a world where peace still has a chance.
Simply put, I have been proving my love for you upon my every rant.
Simply put, I'd have to say that I'm still not even close to the end...
"Smile my love – we are now at the beginning."

Wars of the Mind

The knight I am, constantly battling these endless Wars of the Mind.
Such beautiful rants that have grown attached the acid dripping down my spine.
For decades this soul has been walking and searching for comfort and rest.
And when irony does occur in my life, it's only because I gave it the chance.

The poet I am, constantly ripping off my own shamed and forgotten face.
These endless battles I do fight, within my heart, my soul, my bones and grave.
For so many years this has gone on, and I shall still battle "for you" every day.
You my love – my reader – my inspiration with whom I share my loves and pains.

The demon I am, here laughing with no one at all beside me.
With the ghosts be found the reasons of the constant rage and torment.
For ages I have been beaten for the simple fact that I can take it all.
And forever I shall remain here at war, doing my best to save our souls.

The hero I am not, for I can't even shelter you from this endless war.
I am but a poet that has hidden his heart, behind an open door.
And all of my truths shall remain frozen, upon my every twisted line.
Still I shall remain at your side, battling these endless Wars of the Mind.

The knight I am, still battling my way to be there at your side.
I am many things, millions of creatures and voices in my mind.
Still I stand and battle, doing my best to keep you strong and safe.
Though I am not a hero, still I shall be here at your side every day.

The poet I am, here standing on a ledge and looking down.
For ages I've been out of my mind, somewhere where I couldn't be found.
I am here with you and together we shall survive these endless Wars of the Mind.
So now I believe that I can smile, as we shall all together fall away "so sweetly-departed..."

If it's likely for someone "else" to have a true black-heart.
Then it's likely for me to breathe under water.
"Think about it..."

Extras:

Both the origin of **COUNT YOUR DEAD** and the **WARS OF THE MIND** date back far to the early 2000s when Vocalist/Poet Jonathan W. Haubert and Guitarist Julio C. Salazar formed their first band together in a small town in south Texas. From the beginning Jonathan and Julio were determined to move forward in their careers in Music, no matter what fate may throw their way... Throughout the four year span of shows with their first band and the early writing of the **Wars of the Mind Vol.1 (Upon the Road of Leaves.)** there were times of both joy and grimness alike but they pressed forward through any given trials. Julio, Jonathan and the rest of the band managed to put immense amounts of time, passion, poetry, anger, love, pain and unending effort to write what were some of the best songs of that early time period in their careers in Music and stage. Some of their best songs played mostly live, including titles such as (**Still Bleeding, AnyWay, Gotta Run, RAZOR** and many many more), all of these songs being written during the long nights filled with unrelenting practices, complete devotion, and endless passion. But as time would pass, Jonathan, Julio and the rest of the band would end up parting ways. Jonathan would end up going off to start the relentless writings of the **WARS OF THE MIND** poetry series and beginning his Solo Project entitled **FnQiNu**, which consisted of materials picking up where their previous projects had left off, and Julio would end up taking some time off from music to peruse his degree in Diesel Mechanics. In 2006 after a short break from music, Julio would then jump back into the mix of stage and recording in the early beginnings of **COUNT YOUR DEAD**. So, as fate would have it, circumstances had led to Jonathan and Julio reuniting in the reformation of **COUNT YOUR DEAD** and the recording of their debut album **"No Return"**. While some of the tracks were written as far back as **Count Your Dead**'s earliest formation, others such as **"Bitter Resurrections,""Say When..."** and **"1,000 Miles of Pain"** would serve as new fuel to an already burning fire. And while some songs possess a twistedly sarcastic theme to them, such as **"Flooding Texas"** and **"Bleed Smoke"** do, others contain a more crucial and personal meaning. One of the most personal being **"Release"** which deals with the issues of the acceptance of losing loved ones to death. And many other strong points with the relentless rants such as the ones in **"Poetic Lies"** which speaks of the mindless nonsense which others try to feed to others as truth. Over the years both the songs and the band have progressed and continue to grow still. After the releasing of **Count Your Dead**'s debut album **"NO RETURN,"** the band began the most amazing adventures of its career in the winning of awards, countless live shows, new recordings and the beginning of the up and coming second **COUNT YOUR DEAD** album and the early writing of the next epic chapter in the ongoing series in **WARS OF THE MIND Vol.6 (Another American Poet.)**

Thanks:

I would like to thank my family and friends that have stayed by my side for all these long years of poetry and Heavy Metal. And all my brothers in "COUNT YOUR DEAD" for all these years of great shows and for all of the years of friendships, adventure in recording, stage, and !!HEAVY METAL!! Again I would like to thank you the reader.
For taking this 5th journey into the wars of the mind.
And to everyone who picks up this book. And holds it true to their heart. "I thank you all."

Jonathan W. Haubert: Vocals   **Julio C. Salazar: Guitar**

www.countyourdead.com

"God, Give Me Back My Apathy..."

(*Jonathan W. Haubert*)

Coming Soon:

Wars of the Mind
Vol. 6: (*Another American Poet.*)